What leaders are saying about
The Lens of Leadership . . .

Kevin Scott has earned a reputation for developing leaders. It's why we partnered with ADDO to create Chick-fil-A Leader Academy and why I'd recommend that leaders everywhere read this book. In every chapter of *The Lens of Leadership*, Kevin opens our eyes to see more clearly what we do. When we look through a new lens, we make better decisions, relate to people more effectively, and become better leaders.

David Salyers
Vice President of Growth and Hospitality at Chick-fil-A

Over the last decade, I have watched Kevin effectively lead organizations and teams. He knows how to frame concepts, and he is a master at telling great stories. In this new book, Kevin puts it all together to help leaders see themselves and their jobs in fresh ways. Every leader needs to see more clearly, and this book helps them do just that!

Vince Dooley
Hall of Fame Football Coach, Legendary University of Georgia Coach and Athletic Director

On stages and in board rooms, I've seen Kevin inspire leaders and equip them with tools to take their organizations to the next level. In this book Kevin shares relevant insights that will change your perspective on life and leadership. Read *The Lens of Leadership*, and be prepared to make some significant changes in how you see, how you think, and how you lead!

Ned Bowman
Executive Director of Florida Petroleum Marketers Association

The best leaders live "on purpose," sincerely care about others, and lead with the character and competency to make a meaningful impact. In *The Lens of Leadership*, Kevin Scott opens our eyes to see our challenges with more insight, hope, and courage than before. Every chapter is full of practical and actionable advice about how to put these principles into practice and lead at a higher level. This is a great book!

Brian Cook
CEO of Cook's Pest Control

Over the last decade, Kevin has built a reputation for fresh insights about leadership, and this book may be his best work yet. *The Lens of Leadership* gives us nine areas to see ourselves and our roles differently. I know my personal lens on leadership is much clearer now. Every leader needs to read this book!

Bob Somers
Senior Vice President of Global Sales, Delta Air Lines

Kevin Scott explores nine profound lenses (and lessons) of leadership that are relevant, easy to understand and actionable in his new book, *The Lens of Leadership*. Obviously a gifted author, strategist, and teacher, Kevin is a clear "thought leader." I heartily endorse this terrific book.

Ira Blumenthal
Best Selling Author and Professional Speaker
CEO of The Pat Summitt Leadership Group

Kevin's book is thought-provoking; both wide ranging and practical. Anyone with any organizational responsibility would benefit from reading it.

Frank and Liz Blake
Frank is Former CEO of The Home Depot
Liz is Retired Senior Vice President of Habitat for Humanity Int'l

Effective leaders are always growing, always learning, always eager to sharpen their skills and have a greater impact. In this book, Kevin Scott opens our eyes to see our challenges with more insight, hope, and courage than ever before. Every chapter is full of practical advice about how to implement the principles.

Muhtar Kent
Chairman of the Board, The Coca-Cola Company

THE
LENS
OF LEADERSHIP

NINE STRATEGIC SHIFTS IN PERSPECTIVE

KEVIN PAUL SCOTT
AUTHOR OF *8 ESSENTIAL EXCHANGES*

Scripture passages are from The Holy Bible, English Standard Version. ESV® Text Edition: 2016. Copyright © 2001 by Crossway Bibles, a publishing ministry of Good News Publishers.

ISBN: 978-1-947505-07-0

Published in the United States by Baxter Press, Friendswood, Texas

❧

To Laura,

who has enabled me to see life through a better, clearer lens.

CONTENTS

INTRODUCTION
A CLEARER PERSPECTIVE

To change ourselves effectively, we first had to change our perceptions.
—Stephen R. Covey

60 Minutes correspondent Bill Whitaker watched in amazement. Two ophthalmologists, Doctors Geoff Tabin and Sanduk Ruit, were performing cataract surgeries on dozens of patients in Myanmar. Whitaker asked, "What's it like when the bandage is taken off and that person sees for the first time? Sees you?"

Dr. Ruit answered, "I may have seen it thousands of times, but every time, there's a new tickle there. And I feel like my battery's been recharged."

Dr. Tabin joined in: "I still get such a thrill when people don't expect or realize they're gonna have their sight restored. And then a transformation when they see, and the sort of moment of hesitation, what are they seeing, and then the smile."

The problem of blindness, or at least partial blindness, is an epidemic in Myanmar. Some people have been blind for months, some for years, others for decades. Their primary problem is cataracts, the thickening film on the eye's lens that clouds vision. In the United States, this problem affects mostly older people, but in Myanmar, it's a crisis for virtually every segment of society due to malnutrition and untreated infections.

A surgery that takes only four or five minutes can radically change the trajectory of the person's life. Life expectancy, career opportunities, school involvement for children, and the possibility of having a meaningful family life are all on the line . . . the line between blurred vision and clear sight.

Doctors Ruit and Tabin, with the help of grants from foundations in America, have restored sight to more than 150,000 people in two dozen countries. Each procedure results in a person with a new beginning. A 15-year-old boy had his sight restored and can now read and return to school. His grateful mother realizes her son now has a bright future. She called the doctors "gods." They shrug off such compliments, but Bill Whitaker concludes, "In this room, it certainly seemed they had performed miracles."[1]

Few of us have vision problems severe enough to require surgery, but all of us have problems with sight. We assume the way we see ourselves, our situations, and other people is accurate, but since we're human, our perception is limited . . . and sometimes it's dead wrong![2]

Like most newly married couples, my wife Laura and I have had plenty of moments when we realized we had very different perspectives on situations and people. During our first year of marriage, we planned a dream vacation to Italy. A week before our departure, Laura was nervous, but I was completely relaxed. She was concerned because we hadn't reserved hotel rooms in any of the cities where we were traveling. I planned to just show up and take our chances. Neither of us had voiced our concerns and expectations, but our perceptions were vastly different. To Laura, the vacation was a really big deal. Both of us work hard, and she expected our trip to be something very special, so she wanted to plan every detail and make it perfect. To me, much of the fun of a vacation is the adventure of being spontaneous.

I soon learned ("Earth to newlywed!") that I needed to learn to see things from Laura's perspective. It wasn't that my point of view was wrong, but neither was Laura's. We both were seeing things in a way that felt right and natural, but the good of the marriage depended on our beginning to see things from the other's perspective. Our happiness—and the joy of our vacation—depended on each of us making a "shift" in the way we thought and related to one another.

This book will examine nine "shifts" that all leaders need to consider. After analyzing the shifts addressed in this book, all readers should be able to stand back and see a wider panorama of how the various strategies interconnect and reinforce one another. Most leaders will need to have their prescriptions adjusted to see a bit more clearly. And some, I hope, will discover a fresh, new, even revolutionary perspective they've never seen before.

It is crucial that effective leaders learn to see more clearly. Accurate perception begins with us, yet it doesn't end there. We can't help others see their steps of needed change until we see ourselves more clearly. But after we do, one of our primary responsibilities is then to help our people develop a clearer perception that enables them to contribute with enthusiasm, purpose, and excellence.

Theologian N.T. Wright has taught me that people learn by contrasts. Photographers take care to show mountains against the sky; composers arrange music with rhythmic, melodic, and harmonic contrasts; and painters use perspective, color, and even texture to heighten visual interest. When I think of the communicators I admire, I realize they have mastered the art of painting verbal or written pictures by contrasting goals, values, and purposes. We have insight when we realize we've been thinking *this*, but now we understand *that*; we've been doing *this*, but now we are committed to doing *that*; we've seen ourselves and others through a cloudy lens, but when we wipe off the dust we can see more clearly. In each of the chapters that follow, I'll show the contrast between faulty perspective and a clearer perspective. These insights improve our most intimate relationships with family and friends, and we will apply them to our careers as well. Gaining a clearer, wider, more accurate perspective creates profound changes in every area of life.

How you view things changes how you do things.

PERCEPTION MATTERS

In many organizations, the people who have the greatest impact on customer perception are often the lowest paid and have received the least training. For instance, airlines pay their executives and pilots the highest salaries, but the flight attendants and gate agents have more influence on customer satisfaction. I know this is true because I have firsthand experience.

A few years ago, I spent a week in Bali, Indonesia, working on a book with my coauthor. I took my mother and a friend on the trip. Our meetings on the island paradise were very productive, but when we caught a glimpse of the news, we got concerned. A couple of days before leaving Bali, we saw reports of a massive typhoon slamming into Japan. The first leg of our trip home took us to Singapore, and then we flew about six hours to Narita, an airport just outside Tokyo. When we got off the plane and prepared to board the flight back to the U.S., we learned hundreds of flights had been cancelled in the days before we landed, and the airline was struggling to get people to their destinations. The bad news was that we were on standby. The good news is that we were numbers 11, 12, and 13 on the list, and the gate agent assured us there were plenty of open seats on the flight.

Near the end of the boarding process, the agent began calling the names of people who were on the standby list. She called the first ten names and we started gathering our carry-on items, but we didn't hear another word. I asked the agent if she was ready for us to board. She frowned and shook her head. I explained, "We were told there are plenty of seats on this plane." Again, she shook her head. She explained that cargo from cancelled flights had been loaded on this plane, so even though there were still empty seats, the plane had reached its maximum weight capacity. I pleaded, but she wasn't at all sympathetic. She pointed me to a ticket agent at a booth across the room.

As I approached the ticket agent, she was already scowling. I patiently explained our situation and asked if she could get us on the next flight to the U.S. She looked annoyed, glanced at a schedule, and announced there was nothing available that day. I asked if she would book us on a flight the next day, but she almost barked, "There's nothing I can do. Come back tomorrow. No guarantee."

I had begun the conversation with the ticket agent feeling anxious, but hopeful; I left feeling angry and desperate. She clearly didn't see herself as a representative of an airline that cares about people; she had seen her job as getting the bare facts across to me as quickly as possible. I wish she'd been more resourceful, and I wish she'd had an ounce of empathy. Her perspective made a lot of difference to me, my mother, and my friend.

We got rooms at a hotel near the airport, and I burned up the internet asking for help. When I posted our predicament on Facebook, dozens of friends sent notes of support and encouragement. Several had really good ideas about finding a flight home. Finally, I called the airline's international number, but I had no idea what to expect. Would the person on the other end of the line be as brusque as the lady at the ticket counter? I was pleasantly surprised when this woman turned out to be the epitome of kindness and efficiency. She immediately connected with me on an emotional level. "I'm so sorry this happened to you," she told me. "I'll do everything I can to help." She spent a long time on the phone with me, explaining options and asking which one I preferred. At one point, she asked if she could put me on hold so she could talk to her supervisor. When she came back, she obviously had pulled some strings for me. The next day, the three of us were on flights home . . . business class!

In businesses, nonprofits, and other organizations, leaders often have trouble translating corporate values down to the frontline personnel. In my experience at the airline, the gate agent and the ticket agent obviously saw themselves as dispassionate dispensers of raw data, but the person on the phone in customer service embodied the heart, values, and voice of the company.

Sometimes, however, it's the people at the top who have faulty vision. An owner of an independent grocery store asked to meet with me. He was frustrated . . . *exasperated* might be a better word. He'd had the opportunity to see how Chick-fil-A owner/operators train their employees, and he was amazed at the high level of enthusiasm for even the most mundane tasks in serving customers. His experience with employees was quite the opposite. With a mixture of doom and gloom, he told me, "Kevin, I just can't seem to get it across to my people. They just don't care about doing a great job and making our customers feel special."

> *Their* perception may not have needed changing, but *his* sure did!

I asked, "How do you decide who to hire?"

He smiled weakly, "If people can tie their shoes and utter a complete sentence, I'll give them a job."

His statement instantly told me that the people he hired could have been as sharp as they come, yet he saw them as inept and inefficient. *Their* perception may not have needed changing, but *his* sure did! Undoubtedly, his (unsubstantiated) view of them shaped his communications, his expectations and theirs, and ultimately his employees' relationships with customers who came to the store. His employees became a reflection of how he saw them, and it wasn't pretty.

A LOOK IN THE MIRROR

Perhaps the most important step we can take in gaining a proper perspective is to admit we are, at least to some degree, self-deceived. For a long time, we've been sure we were seeing things clearly (and correctly!), but now we have to face the hard truth that our vision has been somewhat clouded. This is an easy admission for some of us, but others can't stand the idea that their views might not be completely, absolutely accurate!

Virtually all of us see ourselves, our situations, and others through a particular lens:

- Some of us have to be on top. When we don't win, we get really upset. We can't be satisfied until we've trampled the competition. To us, life is a battle. Only one person can be superior, and by definition, others are inferior—so nobody is going to beat us! A few people may admire our tenacity, but others feel used, intimidated, and terrified.

- Some of us long for significance, but we're afraid we really don't matter. We feel like little cogs in a much bigger machine. We try to organize our lives and make calculated decisions so we don't fail (too badly), but we live with the gnawing fear that we'll never measure up. We're sure that we have no detectable impact on the organization. In fact, if we don't show up tomorrow, nobody would even wonder where we were. We're convinced people on our teams put up with us, but we secretly fear they're annoyed by our presence.

- Some of us live for affirmation, and we're terrified we'll be rejected—or worse, ignored. We try to say the right thing, wear the right clothes, go to the right places, and be seen with the right people so others will be impressed with us, but we're always looking over our shoulders. Unless we're the center of the universe (or at least our group of friends or our department), we feel small, devalued, overlooked. We need to always say things and do things so the people above us on the organizational chart notice us, and we expect the people below us to feel honored to have us as their boss.

- Some of us have lost sight of what's valuable. We may have been passionate in the past, but no longer. Perhaps the accumulation of repeated small setbacks has taken a toll, or perhaps a single traumatic event has left us devastated. Either way, we aren't really alive anymore. We're drifting, and not in a good direction. Work is a grind, life is a bore, friendships are fleeting and few, and family life is more of a challenge than a joy.

Drift, boredom, and despair can easily occur if leaders don't continually inject fresh vision and purpose into their people. Although those we oversee often start well, they sometimes don't end well. Consider these common stages:

THE HIGH COST OF LOW ENGAGEMENT

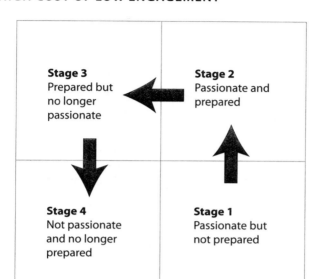

A recent Gallup poll shows that 32% of employees are "engaged" (that is, in Stages 1 and 2), 51% are "not engaged" (Stage 3), and 17% are "actively disengaged" (Stage 4).[3]

Stage 1: Passionate but not prepared.

When people join a company, they're often excited about their new jobs and motivated to prove themselves, but it takes time for them to be trained and equipped so they can really contribute.

Stage 2: Passionate and prepared.

After they've been trained, new hires are often very productive. They're passionate about the company and eager to make the team successful. They're outstanding advocates and recruiters for the company.

Stage 3: Prepared but no longer passionate.

After a period of time, usually a few months to a few years, work can begin to feel stale. Disagreements on the team remain unresolved, resentment builds, others are promoted faster, and some employees become cynical and disengaged. At this stage, they begin to develop alliances based on distrust and doubt, not passion and purpose.

Stage 4: Not passionate and no longer prepared.

If the drift isn't stopped, disgruntled employees develop a faithful following of others who buy into their negative view of life and the company's leaders. In this stage, individuals disconnect from their responsibilities and stop investing in growth. Every good thing the executives do is perceived as a selfish power play, even if done with the most noble motives. In Stage 3, correction was possible, but difficult; it's even more difficult, and almost impossible, for those in Stage 4. Every attempt to help at this point is interpreted as manipulation.

This emphasis on a leader's perception isn't ancillary or irrelevant. The way we see ourselves, the company, our teams, and our purpose makes a world of difference in every aspect of life. Healthy, accurate, positive perception leads to more personal fulfillment, more effective team relationships, better connections with customers and clients, and a more profitable company. How you view things really does change how you do things. And how you do things shapes the culture of a team and can even shape an entire organization.

Employees either contribute to or diminish the productivity of the company . . . at every level. If you ask a CEO how many employees are in each stage, she might say most are in the first two stages: they're excited, and many are trained and productive. Those in the latter two stages may be few, but by that point they are actively poisoning the water. Since we're concentrating on seeing more clearly, we might say they're "the blind leading the blind" into a pit.

If employee drift is not corrected before Stage 3 and 4, the financial consequences can be substantial. For instance, if a CEO identifies twenty people in Stages 3 and 4, and they make an average of $20 an hour, the annual dollar cost to the company is $832,000 (20 x $20 x 2,080 hrs./year). Of course, they get *some* work done, so let's say only half of their time is unproductive. The cost to the organization is still $416,000 annually for those twenty people. In addition, the corporate dysfunction they create diminishes the time and energy of many other employees.

People in Stage 4 become what some leaders call "onboard terrorists." It's bad enough that they lack passion and are unproductive, but even worse is that they show up to work each day trying to figure out how to bring the ship down! In a post about an employee who sabotaged his staff and clients, Dr. David Moffet gives this analysis and stark conclusion:

> "Typically, the Onboard Terrorist is a good employee. They purvey genuinely good business characteristics for a reasonable amount of time [through Stages 1 and 2, and even into 3]. However, when they switch to Terrorist mode, their negative effect on your business seriously outweighs any good they seem to be performing. . . . It is the responsibility of management to identify the Terrorist and deal with them. Sadly, as in the case of true terrorism there is no redemption. A terrorist must be excised. . . . In fact, the process of excision will elevate the office leader in the eyes of the other employees."[4]

In this book, I'm going to look through the lens of the corporate world, but the problems and principles apply to people in every kind of organization and relationship. There are very real benefits of seeing clearly, and there are very real costs of having fuzzy vision:

- The real cost of a faulty perspective in business is lower productivity and profits.

- The real cost of a faulty perspective in nonprofit organizations is less impact on people in need.

- The real cost of a faulty perspective in schools is that teachers and students don't flourish.

- The real cost of a faulty perspective in government is partisanship and gridlock.

- The real cost of a faulty perspective in churches is the failure to transform people and communities.

- The real cost of a faulty perspective in families and friendships is unresolved friction, unrelieved strains, chronic hurt, and resentment.

- The real cost of a faulty perspective in individuals is attempting to use power, approval, control, and possessions to fill up empty lives. It may seem to work for a while, but not for long.

In *Leadership and Self-Deception*, the author describes the powerfully negative feedback loop of being blind:

> "Self-deception is like this. It blinds us to the true causes of problems, and once we're blind, all the 'solutions' we can think of will actually make matters worse. Whether at work or at home, self-deception obscures the truth about ourselves, corrupts our view of others and our circumstances, and inhibits

our ability to make wise and helpful decisions. To the extent that we are self-deceived, both our happiness and our leadership are undermined at every turn."[5]

MY HOPE FOR YOU

In this book, we'll look at how a shift in perspective—looking through a new lens at nine aspects of leadership—can make a significant difference in every aspect of our lives, how we lead our teams, and the impact we have on our customers. The first—and most important—aspect

Your skills matter, but you'll have a far greater impact if you relate to your work and other people with a beautiful blend of passion and humility.

of leadership is *purpose*, and this insight clarifies all the others. Your skills matter, but you'll have a far greater impact if you relate to your work and other people with a beautiful blend of passion and humility.

We will also see that the four stages I've outlined aren't set in stone. They don't have to end in disaster! There's another path—a much better one—after Stage 2. Instead of drifting downward into boredom and cynicism, people can become lifelong learners, stay sharp, and continue to grow. When this happens, they become incredible assets to the company, and with the wisdom they gain over time, they're also happier, more present with their families, more creative, and more satisfied. These people also form alliances, but not built on mutual resentments toward those above them. They craft bonds that become lasting, strong friendships. Over the years, their sense of purpose becomes deeper, stronger, and even more compelling.

In our company, we've redefined the term "ROI." Instead of *return on investment*, we talk constantly about *return on impact*. Investment can be sterile, but the pursuit of impact always requires sharpening our purpose and serving others with genuine care. We want employees with this kind of commitment, and we know it starts with our leadership.

The goal of good leadership, however, is not merely retention of productive employees. Some of the most gifted leaders I know value their employees' engagement with customers more than their tenure. This corporate priority puts the emphasis on enthusiasm, empathy, and excellence. If highly motivated people believe they can start their own businesses or find a better job, good leaders send them off with a celebration untainted by resentment. And the leaders then recruit, train, and empower new employees to be just as engaged and just as effective.

Your people are in one of the stages (including the possibility of staying sharp after Stage 2 and not running off the rails). As a leader, you're in one of the stages, too. Be humble enough to realize that you, like everyone else, need a new set of lenses to help you see more clearly. Even if you've drifted into resentment, it's never too late to see more clearly and then help the people who report to you get back on track. Some leaders, however, may require more than a new set of lenses: they may need Doctors Tabin and Ruit to perform surgery!

At the end of this Introduction and each subsequent chapter, you'll find a few questions designed to stimulate your reflection and propel group discussion. Don't rush through these. Learning to see clearly requires honesty—sometimes painful honesty—and plenty of encouragement as you and others take steps forward.

It is a narrow mind which cannot look at a subject
from various points of view.
—George Eliot

TAKE A LOOK . . .

1.   Describe a time when someone treated you as an annoyance, and then describe a time when someone treated you with kindness and respect. What do you imagine are some differences in how each of those people saw themselves, their jobs, and you?

2.   What are some factors that can cause someone to "run off the rails" after Stage 2? What happens to those people personally in Stages 3 and 4? What is their effect on others?

3.   How can leaders help people stay sharp and become lifelong learners after Stage 2? What is their "return on impact" for the company?

4. How would you define and describe the "real cost of a faulty perspective" in your company or organization?

5. What do you hope to get out of reading this book?

CHAPTER 1
PURPOSE

We won't be distracted by comparison if we are captivated by purpose.
—Bob Goff

Today the American corporate world is suffering from an epidemic of apathy. A 2017 study by Deloitte Services LP revealed that U.S. companies spent over $100 billion on training and $1 billion to promote employee engagement, but only thirteen percent of employees are described as "passionate" about their work. Almost two-thirds are "half-hearted" and disengaged, and the rest, almost one in four, fall in the netherworld between passionate and disengaged.

The study identified three distinct characteristics of passionate employees: (1) long-term commitment to making a difference; (2) active pursuit of new challenges to accelerate personal development; and (3) the desire to build relationships based on trust. Perhaps surprisingly, only half of executives and senior management qualified as passionate and engaged.

The task of employers is complicated by the rapidly changing corporate culture and technological advances. John Hagel, managing director for Deloitte, observes,

"Worker engagement may no longer be sufficient for performance improvement. In an environment of mounting performance pressure and increasing unpredictability, companies need a workforce that embraces challenge. Worker passion is becoming a key attribute for employees with the skill set that will contribute to sustained performance improvement for companies in increasingly competitive markets."[6]

When we think of "purpose," our minds naturally go in one of two directions: our personal purpose or our organization's corporate purpose. Both are essential. We'll focus first on the reason each of us gets up every morning, and we'll see how our purpose propels us to be more passionate and engaged at work.

Effective leaders realize it's not enough to dictate a predetermined corporate purpose. They want to help all the people on their team articulate their purpose in life. Employees are engaged when they are prepared and passionate about their work and live with a compelling sense of purpose in every area of their lives. Passion is the natural result of connecting their tasks to their purpose.

Many people perceive purpose to be elusive and exclusive, but leaders need to see that it's both accessible and attainable.

THE REAL THING

Passion, energy, commitment, and optimism don't just happen. People don't produce those qualities out of thin air at *any* level of an organization. Some people are naturally optimistic, and others can fake it for a while, but if those characteristics are going to last, they must be rooted deep in a person's sense of meaning . . . of purpose . . . of a deep desire to make a difference.

In virtually every book and seminar on business, the "experts" insist that a crucial step for any company is to craft a vision statement. My experience in working with CEOs, managers, and employees is that most people see their corporate vision statement as superfluous crap. It may look nice in a frame in the boardroom or on the website, but it often has virtually no bearing on how people make choices, relate to each other, and engage customers and clients. Quite often, the top executives spend hours crafting a vision statement, and they feel great about it, but the mid-level managers only give lip service to it, and it seldom affects the frontline employees at all. Those outside the executive offices hardly pretend to buy into the vision statement. It's like the wallpaper in the restroom: it's there, but no one really notices.

We need a calling that draws out our best ideas, our creativity, and our most tenacious effort. We need a compelling sense of *purpose*.

We all need something more than a vision statement, something worth living for, something that inspires passion. We need a calling that draws out our best ideas, our creativity, and our most tenacious effort. We need a compelling sense of *purpose*.

Some people who read the preceding paragraph feel unsure, even insecure or confused. They may have read a dozen books on vision, mission, and purpose, but no matter how hard they try, they can't quite put their finger on the exact thing that captures their hearts. This problem can be amplified if they come from a church background. They've heard all about the great leaders in the Bible: Moses coming down from Sinai with the Ten Commandments, Joshua leading God's people into the Promised Land, Nehemiah rebuilding the walls of Jerusalem, Peter standing up at Pentecost and launching a movement that now claims more than a third of the inhabitants of the planet, and on and on. Nothing they can imagine compares to any of those accounts!

But it gets worse for those people: the books and sermons all seem to promise that at some glorious moment, God (or some other voice) will break into their reality to reveal a unique and grand purpose in life, but they're still waiting for him to appear. When such people hear that they need a sense of purpose, they groan in despair because they're convinced they'll never have one. It's always just beyond their grasp. It only makes things worse when they hear other individuals speak enthusiastically about how they've found their purpose and how it's made all the difference to them. The enthusiasm is intended to encourage the ones who are struggling, but too often, the listeners feel deflated instead. The gap between the lofty promise of purpose and their personal and pervasive sense of emptiness leaves the despairing individuals feeling like second-class people.

Others (and I'm among them) are insecure for a different reason. We believe we've identified *why* our lives matter, but we don't always feel confident sharing that information. We don't want to sound arrogant, or more likely, we're afraid we'll fail to live up to our purpose and look foolish to those we've told—especially if we're young.

For a long time, I had trouble owning my purpose statement: "To inspire people today to impact tomorrow." Before this purpose crystalized, I learned what it's like to have a cloudy reason to live, and after it became clear, I understood the reluctance of telling people about my purpose. I feared looking like an idiot if I crashed and burned.

Either of those problems, confusion or fear, robs us of a compelling reason to get up in the morning, yet we find some sense of safety in the insecurity. If we're not clear or not bold in telling people, we avoid the risk of being embarrassed when we fall short. It's when we confidently articulate our purpose that we find ourselves in the spotlight, or maybe under a microscope, for everyone to clearly see whether we've succeeded or failed.

A study by Nick Craig and Scott Snook of the Harvard Business School found that not even twenty percent of leaders and managers have a clear personal purpose, and even fewer can articulate their purpose. They distinguish between an organization's vision statement and the individuals' sense of purpose. Virtually all companies, nonprofits, and other organizations have some form of a vision or mission statement, but Craig and Scott have found that corporate success is hindered by executives and employees whose personal purpose is unclear. They explain:

> "Your leadership purpose is who you are and what makes you distinctive. Whether you're an entrepreneur at a start-up or the CEO of a Fortune 500 company, a call center rep or a software developer, your purpose is your brand, what you're driven to achieve, the magic that makes you tick. It's not *what* you do, it's *how* you do your job and *why*—the strengths and passions you bring to the table no matter where you're seated. Although you may express your purpose in different ways in different contexts, it's what everyone close to you recognizes as uniquely you and would miss most if you were gone."[7]

We are inundated by competing messages—invitations and challenges to value one purpose more than another. We're given plenty of reasons to make value judgments: if we follow this or that path we'll be happier, more fulfilled, richer, and more successful and popular. It's hard to resist promises like that! But purpose is deeper . . . much deeper. Your statement of meaning doesn't have to be totally unique, but it needs to tap into your strengths, desires, and vision of what difference it will make as it becomes a reality. Listen to people who have a purpose statement, read about others who have one, and then craft your own. Yours doesn't need to sound like any you've ever read or heard . . . as long as you own it and it motivates you to take action.

THE SYNERGY OF PURPOSES

Our individual purpose, though, is never in a vacuum. We are relational creatures, and we function well only when we're connected to people who inspire us, challenge us, or have strengths in areas where we're deficient. My business partner, Garrett Gravesen, fits that description well, except that he and I are very similar in many ways. We're both driven, relational, and intuitive, so I originally assumed we would be a world-beating team.

I vividly recall a conversation with another good friend, Ike Reighard, who had much more experience with partnerships and teams. After listening to Garrett and me paint a glowing picture of how we were planning to conquer the world, Ike leaned across his desk and told us, "If the two of you aren't careful, you'll be doing prison ministry from the inside!" After we recovered from the shock of his statement, he explained, "I'm not talking about intentionally having wrong motives or intending to commit a crime. My point is that if you don't find some people who are gifted in managing details, you're going to miss something—something important—and find yourself in big trouble."

Garrett and I listened. We recruited people with gifts, talents, and purposes that complement ours. Those people have enhanced our effectiveness, and maybe just as importantly, they've kept us out of trouble (most of the time, anyway). Neither Garrett nor I have an ounce of passion about accounting. We want to dream about the big picture, present concepts in compelling ways, and see lives changed. But if we didn't rely on people who love to handle the details of finances, we probably would have missed paying some bills and taxes. Ike's blunt honesty helped us staff our organization to fill in the holes in our leadership. It was the first time I realized the utter importance of people whose personalities, talents, and purposes are so different from mine.

Failing to value others' contributions isn't just ineffective; it can be deadly. One of the most memorable disasters in the last generation occurred on January 28, 1986, when the Challenger space shuttle blew up 73 seconds after liftoff at Cape Canaveral. The weather that morning was clear and cold. The day before, engineers had voiced their concerns to Morton Thiokol, the contractor who had constructed the solid rocket motor. They realized that the O-rings on the fuel tanks hadn't been tested in the low temperatures that were predicted. Thiokol's chief engineer, Allan McDonald, refused to give his okay to launch. That should have been enough to put the brakes on the flight, but NASA officials overruled him and gave the green light anyway.[8] Anyone who was alive in the mid-80s, and those who have since seen the startling images, will never forget the catastrophe that resulted because of competing purposes.

In a book about the Challenger tragedy, author Diane Vaughan describes the culture of NASA as driven by performance. Her research found the explosion could be attributed to "institutional banalities" in which "deviance" from normal decision-making processes had become institutionalized, resulting in "an incremental descent into poor judgment." The crash was technically a failure of the O-rings in the cold morning air, but much more, it was a failure of NASA executives to listen to McDonald's concerns.[9]

In 1962 when President Kennedy gave our country the challenge to "go to the moon in this decade," NASA was first stunned, then energized and dedicated. Few clearer, more compelling corporate purposes have ever been uttered. However, the pressure to meet that deadline caused scientists and engineers to cut corners. Some of the early rockets in the space program had abysmal failure rates of more than one explosion for every four launches. The first astronauts understood the rocket roaring to life under them had a 25 percent chance of blowing up instead of propelling them into space.[10]

Having a clear, driving purpose is a good start, but it isn't enough on its own. We need people around us who have complementary purposes, very different strengths, and the willingness to speak up . . . and we need to listen to them. It's foolish to adopt someone else's purpose statement instead of crafting our own, but it is equally foolish to think a personal purpose statement makes us superheroes who need no help from anyone. We need perception about our own calling and purpose, and we need perception about the inestimable value of those around us whose skills and interests are very different from ours.

> **We need people around us who have complementary purposes, very different strengths, and the willingness to speak up . . . and we need to listen to them.**

Some team members are very goal-oriented, driven, and determined. They usually have a very clear purpose, and they marshal all their resources to fulfill it. Others lack bravado, but they play a pivotal role. Their goal is to help the team succeed, perhaps by managing risk and reducing chaos. They seem to be reactors instead of actors, but their strengths are valuable to everyone on the team—especially those who are so driven they often steamroll people and overlook details.

Let me be clear: everyone should specify a personal purpose that motivates us no matter where or how we serve, and then we need to figure out how our personal purpose fits into the larger purposes of our organization and team. Both steps are critical. When either one is absent or unclear, frustration is inevitable. But when both are clear and operative, our passion is energized, we're creative, and we know our lives count.

WHO, WHAT, AND WHY

The first step in identifying your purpose in life is to slow down and give yourself time to reflect on what makes you tick. If you're young, you need to realize that time and experience will probably clarify your purpose, but even now, you probably have a good idea of what lights your fire.

Notice the activities, relationships, and situations that bring out the best in you. When do people sit up and notice your contribution? Conversely, when do you feel out of place, unmotivated, and confused about your role? If you can identify both ends of the spectrum—passionate and bored, thrilled and afraid, energized and apathetic—you'll have a good head start to zeroing in on your purpose.

One of the most important elements of our purpose is the *why* question. Yes, we want to make a difference, but what drives that desire? We all have mixed motives. (If you don't think so, go back to the Introduction and read about self-deception!) Do we genuinely want to use all our talents and experiences to serve people, or do we really want to be noticed and applauded, to dominate others, or to control people and situations? Part of the task in clarifying purpose is to acknowledge our very good and noble motives to accomplish something bigger than ourselves, and to be honest about the less-than-noble reasons we want to succeed. Our purpose should always focus on adding value to the lives of others, not primarily our financial gain, the applause of others, or the power we'll have if we climb higher in the organization.

A true purpose should always extend beyond ourselves; it describes the impact we want to have on others. Purpose is different from goals. Goals are usually self-focused, and they are usually time-limited.

For instance, we might plan to lose ten pounds in two months, to begin saving and investing $300 each month, or to set the alarm twenty minutes earlier so we have time to plan our day and perhaps ask for God's help in the tasks we're anticipating. We can have many goals, but we can only have one driving, compelling, soul-inspiring sense of purpose. Our goals, though, aren't independent of our purpose. The deeper motivation to accomplish our goals for health, money, time, and anything else is to equip us to be more effective in fulfilling our overarching purpose in life.

When we have a sense of purpose, we connect even the most mundane tasks to the broader, more meaningful outcomes. For instance, I don't enjoy doing the myriad of details it takes to run a company. It doesn't excite me to analyze budgets, reconcile bank statements, and make sure we have enough toilet paper left in the bathrooms! But I know those things must be done for our company to function properly, and a fully functioning company allows me to fulfill the reason I exist. I don't think I'll ever love doing the mundane tasks of leading a company, but I don't resent them any longer because I now understand how each one plays an important role in helping the organization be successful.

Executives and team leaders who help employees connect their daily tasks to the purpose of providing value to their customers have unlocked one of the most important keys to leadership. Those who excel at customer service have inspired their people to connect everything they do, even mailroom and accounting tasks, to customer satisfaction.

MARKERS

How can you tell if you have a purpose that has captured your heart and is making a difference in the lives of others? It's not that hard. Here are some markers:

- People with purpose aren't among the demoralizing statistics in the epidemic of apathy. They really care . . . about people, about making a contribution, and about excellence. They connect with others on an emotional level. They don't use people as rungs on their ladder of success, and they don't ignore others' needs, hopes, and dreams. The Bible says these people "rejoice with those who rejoice and weep with those who weep." [11]

- Purpose compels people's actions to match their words. They don't just have a vision statement on the wall or a purpose statement on their LinkedIn page. Their choices and relationships are shaped by what they say they value.

- Insecure, undirected people may lack internal drive because they don't know why they're doing what they do each day, or they may feel insecure and try to compensate by becoming very rigid and inflexible. People with a clear purpose understand the complexities of the process. They remain highly motivated and determined, yet they realize there might be many paths to reach that purpose.

- At particular stages in life, especially when we're young, purpose evolves as it takes shape and is clarified. A few people know even in high school what their lives will be about every day until they die, but most of us require a lot of time, and plenty of trial and error, until we can say, "*This* is why I get up every morning. *This* is the impact I want to have on others, this organization, and the people we serve." As I've mentioned, my problem wasn't a lack of clarity about my purpose; my problem was a lack of courage to speak it and live by it. My waffling caused me to say yes to a lot of opportunities that were good, but not right on target. There was always, of course, a cost: by agreeing to the merely good option, I missed some truly great opportunities.

- People with purpose sense that our lives matter far beyond ourselves. An egocentric lifestyle isn't optional. When our purpose is self-generated, it is necessarily self-limiting: it becomes all about our success, our fame, our power, our wealth, our ability to control people and situations. Don't get me wrong. There's nothing inherently evil or sordid about having money, approval, or power, as long as they are secondary—the results of a purpose that is focused on serving others and making their lives better in some tangible way. Philosophy may be of some assistance in helping people understand what life is about, but I've found spirituality to be an even better source.

Professor and author Os Guinness uses the term "calling" to describe how a God-given purpose affects every aspect of our lives. In *The Call*, Guinness writes: "God calls us to himself so decisively that everything we are, everything we do, and everything we have is invested with a special devotion and dynamism lived out as a response to his summons and service."[12]

You may have a different source of truth, security, and meaning derived from philosophy or another of the world's faiths. I'm not trying to argue out of your source. I'm only insisting that all of us need a source that's far bigger, deeper, and grander than ourselves.

- Purpose helps us see challenges in a different way. In *The Art of the Good Life*, Rolf Dobelli describes his philosophy about coping with mundane activities such as paying a hotel bill or his taxes. He writes, "Living a good life has a lot to do with interpreting facts in a constructive way." To prevent the "sting" of receiving a high hotel bill that might ruin the end of a romantic weekend, he "precommits" to pay the bill when he checks in. And instead of fretting about paying taxes that can seem exorbitant, he focuses on the benefits of living in a free culture in a beautiful city. Enjoyment is, in Dobelli's view, the direct result in having a more positive perspective on bills, taxes, difficult people, traffic, and other annoyances.[13]

Dobelli also differentiates "enjoyment" and "meaning." In an interview, he explained an exercise he conducted with a test group. He asked them to rate their enjoyment of each of a list of activities on scale of 1 to 10. Many of the people rated eating a piece of chocolate as a 9 or a 10, while getting a master's degree was much lower on the enjoyment scale. But when he asked them to rate those same activities according to meaning, the numbers were very different. I think we'd all agree that even though getting an advanced degree is often grueling and takes years, it has far more meaning than eating a piece of chocolate.

Too often, we value enjoyment over meaning, so we flip from activity to activity to find a moment of joy instead of appreciating that an investment in meaning has far higher returns. Enjoyment isn't wrong; it's just not as deep, lasting, or motivating as finding true meaning. When we look back on what has made our lives rich and strong, we almost invariably point to the hard-fought accomplishments that gave us a deeper sense that our lives count.

- Purpose—or the lack of purpose—has very real effects on health and longevity. A study of 6000 people conducted by Patrick Hill, an assistant professor of psychology at Carleton University, found "people with a sense of purpose had a 15 percent lower risk of death, compared with those who said they were more or less aimless. And it didn't seem to matter when people found their direction. It could be in their 20s, 50s or 70s." The study considered other factors that affect longevity: age, gender, emotional well-being, and others. "A sense of purpose trumped all that." Hill asserts that purpose provides a "compass or lighthouse that provides an overarching aim and direction in day-to-day lives." The article about the study concludes, "Purposeful individuals may simply lead healthier lives, . . . but it also could be that a sense of purpose protects against the harmful effects of stress."[14]

The failure to identify and clarify our purpose, then, increases stress and can have significantly detrimental effects on our health. Unrelieved stress produces a wide range of physical, social, and psychological problems, from headaches to suicide. We can't avoid all stress, but having a sense of purpose relieves at least some of the causes of stress, and in addition, helps us cope more effectively with the rest. Hill's study points to an important conclusion: not having a sense of purpose can ruin your health . . . and contribute to an early death.

- Perhaps the clearest mark of an authentic, carefully uncovered purpose is that it clearly articulates *why* we exist, *where* we devote our energies and talents, and *how* we stay motivated during the dry and difficult periods when it looks like we've hit dead ends. If purpose is self-directed, setbacks feel very personal and devastating, but if we live for something greater than ourselves, we can learn from our difficulties and redirect our efforts to fulfill our God-given destiny.

THE IMPORTANCE OF PURPOSE

When we examine every aspect of life through the lens of a transcendent purpose, we're thrilled and thankful when we experience success, and we don't give up when we face roadblocks or criticism. We're open to constructive feedback because we know we always have room to grow, and we have the wisdom to filter out unfounded judgments that are meant to crush us. We will always have to deal with both. Those who truly support us tell us the truth even when it's hard to hear, and when we live for something bigger than ourselves, cynics will try to tear us down. Far too often, we listen to the wrong voices.

You can be successful in the world's eyes without having a sense of purpose, but you won't be fulfilled without one. Wealth and status aren't necessarily signs of a compelling purpose. Plenty of people have made a lot of money, climbed high in their organizations, and wielded power over others, yet their success is entirely self-directed and self-generated. Some of them eventually come to a point where they wonder what their lives have been about. (They call it a midlife crisis.) But it's never too late to dig deeper and find a reason to live that's more gratifying than our bank accounts, titles on the corporate letterhead, or the number of friends on Facebook. My advice to young people is to start early to identify their purpose, and to those who are older, don't wait another day.

- If you're young, don't settle for a lukewarm, undefined reason to get up every day. Take the time and effort to identify why you were put on earth.

- If you're in your 30s or 40s and you've been spinning your wheels until now, look beyond money, power, or a title. Start now to figure out what really matters and how you can make a difference in the lives of others.

- Even if you've already reached the most productive years and your family responsibilities are very demanding, it's not too late to find a deeper motivation to go to work each day and identify better values to impart to your growing children.

- And if you're approaching the "end game" of your career, you still have a lot to give to those around you. Maybe you realize you've lived for yourself, and perhaps you've messed up pretty badly, but it's never too late to believe that God has something meaningful for you to do. You may not start an organization that will change the direction of thousands of lives, but you can volunteer to help in one of those organizations. Your experience, even your failures and heartaches, give you a wealth of wisdom to share with people in need.

Most people experience a "sweet spot" when they find an organization that has a purpose very similar to their own. I've met a number of Chick-fil-A franchise owners who joined forces with the company because the corporate culture is so powerfully other-centered. The company doesn't just have its purpose statement framed on the wall in a boardroom or posted on their website. Their purpose pervades every aspect of corporate life—they really care about other-centered outcomes. Chick-fil-A is unapologetically spiritual in its purpose: "To glorify God by being a faithful steward of all that is entrusted to us and to have a positive influence on all who come into contact with Chick-fil-A."

Sometimes an individual purpose changes a person even if the organization doesn't share his or her perceptions. Louise is a young woman who was a department manager for a healthcare company. The corporate culture was overtly profit-driven, and the executives constantly beat the drum of efficiency and revenues. Louise bought into the culture hook, line, and sinker. From her start as an intern at the company through her first decade of employment, she was far more devoted to career advancement than to having a positive impact on those around her—and they knew it.

One day a colleague had the guts to have an honest conversation with Louise. He pointed out the stress she was putting on those who worked for her, and he assured her they would all be happier and more productive if she had a different outlook. Louise bristled at the suggestion that she wasn't a good manager, but over several more conversations, her defiance began to melt. It took months of soul-searching, but she gradually realized her drive, her passion for excellence, and her grim determination to succeed had nothing to do with improving the lives of others. She thought those qualities were her greatest strengths, but she began to see they were symptoms of a camouflaged problem.

She studied, read, and talked to people who seemed happier in their jobs—and whose employees weren't afraid of them. Still, she wasn't sure what a different purpose would do. Would she lose her edge? Would people take advantage of her?

Louise's friend helped her craft a new purpose statement. It was simple, but it was radically different: "To help others, especially those on my team, become successful and fulfilled." She realized this statement might change nothing, yet it had the potential to change everything. She had thought about leaving the company because she couldn't stand living in the tension of her own creation. She was determined to stay in her job, maintain the same corporate quotas and goals, and keep the same team. However, her motivation, her way of relating, her response to success and failure, and her demeanor would be very different.

At first, her team didn't trust her willingness to change. Later, one of them told her, "When you came in and announced your new purpose statement, I thought it was a load of BS. I was sure you had read an article about 'how to manipulate your team more effectively,' and if anything, you were going to be more skilled at intimidating and confusing us." But this guy and the rest of the team began to see genuine differences. For one thing, when Louise occasionally reverted back to her old style of leadership and barked at them, she apologized and asked them for honest feedback. Over time, her new sense of purpose didn't cause her department to fall apart. Instead, the new levels of trust and affirmation enabled the team to be far more productive . . . and those who had feared her actually began to consider her a friend.

We often find great examples in the world of sports. Few careers are as competitive as coaching college football. We sometimes hear stories of coaches who demand too much of their staff and players, but a few of them truly inspire the people around them. In a locker room talk just before the 2017 championship game between Clemson and Alabama,

Clemson's coach Dabo Sweeney told his players, "Let the light that shines in you be brighter than the light that shines on you." Sweeney didn't suggest that fame is evil and to be avoided; he was saying that there's something much more important than public acclaim. His message was clear: No amount of success and fame was as important as the impact his players have on others by their character and courage. That's not a bad purpose statement for any of us.

When we look through the correct lens, we see that purpose isn't elusive. Instead, we see how each of us can clarify and leverage our purpose to make our lives more meaningful.

If you have a purpose in which you can believe,
there's no end to the amount of things you can accomplish.
—*Marian Anderson*

TAKE A LOOK . . .

1.   Why do you think only half of executives and senior management qualify as passionate and engaged, and fewer than twenty percent of corporate leaders have a clear, personal purpose statement?

2. Here are a few questions that might help clarify your sense of purpose:

- When you were young, what activities did you enjoy? Which ones brought out the best in you? Describe two or three of the most memorable of these activities.

- As you grew up, who did you admire during your adolescent and early adult years? When did you feel most useful and fulfilled? Describe two or three of those times.

- Who believes in you? How would that person (or those people) describe your positive impact on people? Do you agree or disagree with their perceptions? Explain your answer.

- In your life today, what recurring situations and relationships bring out your best? Which ones sap your energy and enthusiasm?

3. Take a shot at writing your personal purpose statement. (Realize it will probably be recrafted a time or two in the future, but do your best to write something now that captures your desire to have an impact on others.)

4. To what extent is your purpose being fulfilled already? What is hindering it? How does it fit with your organization's vision statement?

CHAPTER 2
PRIORITY

Remember that if you don't prioritize your life someone else will.
—Greg McKeown

I n business and our personal lives, we frequently use the word *priorities*. However, Greg McKeown studied this word and came to a surprising conclusion. In his book, *Essentialism: The Disciplined Pursuit of Less*, he observes, "The word *priority* came into the English language in the 1400s. It was singular. It meant the very first or prior thing. It stayed singular for the next five hundred years. Only in the 1900s did we pluralize the term and start talking about *priorities*. Illogically, we reasoned that by changing the word we could bend reality." [15]

This insight isn't irrelevant. On any given day, if I look at the to-do list on my phone's Notes app, I see several things I need to accomplish. The items are listed as I thought of them over the past few days and put them on today's calendar—not in any order of importance. If I can check off eight of the nine things by evening, I generally view the day as successful and feel pretty good about myself. The problem for me (and I suspect I'm not alone) is that the one thing I didn't do might be the most important thing I needed to do. I had priorities, but not a single priority.

One task that has been on my list for about three weeks is to write a letter to thank someone who has consistently believed in me and recently encouraged me deeply. A conversation with him several weeks before I started this chapter was life-giving and life-changing. His input has shaped my life and the direction of our company. Why am I procrastinating? It's not because I don't appreciate him. Quite the opposite: It's because I appreciate him so much that I want my words to reflect the depth of my gratitude. I don't want to mess it up! The letter will take time, thought, and vulnerability. It's a lot easier to do the other eight things that require so much less of me, so I allow each day's attention to my multiple priorities to supersede the one priority that's supremely important. The longer I keep putting it off, the easier it gets to put it off again . . . and again. After a while, it becomes embarrassing to send a letter that should have been sent soon after the conversation. Sooner or later, the reasons for not writing outweigh the reasons for writing, and it drops off the list completely.

Many people perceive priorities to be too many and too messy, but leaders need to see that identifying a single priority is the key to unlocking their effectiveness.

VISION AND ACTION

Even after we have crafted a fantastic statement, our stated purpose can erode due to friction of competing pressures, and we get distracted by too many good options. We live in a stress-filled world, pushed and pulled all day every day. We need a way to maintain our perspective. We need a lens to see what's most important. Our purpose charts a course and paints a picture of a desired future; our priority at any given moment sharpens our focus and steels our resolve to take the next step to fulfill it.

A few months ago, our company was in a very busy season. Over several days, I talked to our team about the paramount importance of retaining existing clients, following up leads to acquire new clients, entering and managing data so we could serve our clients more effectively, adding new people to our team, transitions in responsibilities, and a few other important matters. As I addressed each topic with our team, I either explicitly or implicitly communicated: "This is *the most important thing* for you to focus on!" At the end of the second day, one of the women shook her head and told me, "I don't have time to do everything at the maximum level. Everything can't be of 'ultimate importance.' I need your help: of all these important things, which one is *most* important?" She put her finger on the need for singularity of priority.

As I meet with people, I see the same problem of assigning ultimate importance to too many goals. This usually produces one of two outcomes in team members: they believe "everything is crucial," which makes them feel driven, frustrated, and frantic; or they come to the opposite conclusion that "nothing is crucial," which makes them passive, disconnected, and inefficient.

When leaders fail to sort the important from the urgent, many people on their teams work hard because they want to be "good team players," and they resent anyone who "isn't as committed" to the cause. Some people remain doggedly loyal to an overcommitted boss, but most eventually become exhausted. They've missed so many deadlines that the next one seems pointless. After a while, their attitude slides from eager to skeptical to cynical. They see their boss as too demanding and out of touch, so their priority becomes protecting themselves. Also, they spend more time trying to manage their manager than working on tasks. Every attempt by the manager to get them moving is interpreted as manipulation, so the team member resists and remains passive.

THE RIGHT ORDER

Purpose shows us when to say yes, and priority reveals when to say no. On any day, on any team, and in any organization, there are too many opportunities for the time we have. Setting our priority enables us to say no to good things, maybe very good things, that aren't the absolute best thing in which we can invest our time and talents.

A clear priority enables us to say yes or no, but it also helps us determine the order of our "yeses." For instance, I am committed to spend time with my team, my friends, my clients, my wife, and my extended family, yet only one of those is my priority. Yes, they all relate to my purpose, "To inspire people today to impact tomorrow," but Laura is most important. If I invest my heart in all those except Laura, I will have missed everything.

> Purpose shows us when to say yes, and priority reveals when to say no.

She's not just one more item on my list. She's number one. That doesn't diminish the others in any way. They're also important; they just can't be most important.

When we define a priority for a specific day, week, or month, we realize something has to give. We can't do everything we'd like to do, and we can't give ourselves at the same level for all people all the time. We need wisdom to know how much time and energy to devote to competing desires and demands.

On an organizational level, the best companies identify their top priority during a time or season, yet most executives live with a myriad of "most important" goals. For a few years, the priority of our company wasn't clear. We lived on the edge, so to bring in revenue and become known, we said yes far too often. As a result, our attention was scattered, our brand was diluted, our team ran in different directions, our clients were confused, and we had to continually explain who we were. (Sometimes giving answers even added to the confusion). I spent too much time putting out fires . . . fires we had inadvertently set by being unclear about our purpose and priority. People who visited our website often went away thinking, "They sound like a really cool company, but I have no idea what they actually do for their customers and clients." That's not a good thing for potential clients to say about a company and its brand! We thought we were being reasonable by being so broad. Instead, because we refused to define and limit the services we offered, we appeared to be unreasonable and unfocused.

The real cost of communicating conflicting priorities is that our team became confused and demotivated. They're wonderful people who were giving all they had every day, but we didn't provide enough clarity for them to connect everything they did to our purpose and priority. We sent mixed messages, and those messages were received and internalized.

An individual and an organization can have many goals, but only one of them is supremely important at any given time. When we fail to identify the priority, we feel distressed, and we confuse those who report to us.

In an article for Brighton Leadership Group, the author advises leaders to "Get Rid of Stupid." She writes, "Many activities, reports and goals are orbiting your organizational planet without connection to the current priority. They are left over from a past priority and are taking resources away from what matters now. We hold on to things, to habits, to beliefs, to people, to processes, to ideas and to activities that don't contribute to success. Stupid means lacking in common sense. Use common sense and get rid of what is no longer contributing to accomplishing the priority. Stop the stupid!"[16] This simple (and very direct) advice is, of course, easier said than done. "Stopping the stupid" requires us to make some hard and uncomfortable decisions.

With this insight, and looking through a new perspective, we come to a challenging conclusion: If fewer than twenty percent of executives, managers, and employees have a clearly articulated purpose, and of those, when only a small percentage can identify their priority at the moment and connect it to their purpose, that leaves an awful lot of us much work to do to figure out what makes us tick and order our to-do list to get the most out of our time!

Fuzzy perception has a big influence on the bottom line and the corporate culture. Warwick Business School professors Simon Collinson and Melvin Jay studied the largest 200 companies in the world to determine the impact of having an unclear priority. They concluded that unnecessary complexity caused by the gradual accumulation of too many competing priorities "is slowing companies down, costing them on average 10 percent of their profits and harming employee morale."[17]

A clear purpose enables leaders to save time and resources because they have a grid to determine their priority. They can more readily say no to a lot of good ideas (and all the bad ones) so they can focus on the main thing. This not only saves time; it also streamlines work, keeps employees focused on what matters most, and almost certainly makes a difference on the bottom line. The effort to keep a clear priority, then, has a positive ROI—in both senses of the term.

CONSTANT STRUGGLE

Every leader struggles to keep a focused eye on the priority of the organization. The first time I was invited as a guest on Fox Business (in 2014) was to comment on the recently released Amazon Fire Phone. It was created to compete with Apple's iPhone and Samsung's Galaxy. Even with the business brilliance of Jeff Bezos, Amazon pursued a product that took them away from their central purpose and priority. It was a bomb. By the end of the year, Amazon was selling their phone for 99 cents with a two-year contract. A review by C/Net sardonically notes, "There are times when being the first person with a new gadget will elicit cheers and envy—like outside New York's Fifth Avenue Apple Store, surrounded by applauding salespeople, curious fans and gawking media. Then there's buying the Amazon Fire Phone. . . . It became an uncharacteristic and high-profile failure for a top tech company known for thrilling customers and boldly expanding into new markets."[18] I'm a big fan of Amazon, but even the best companies can get distracted and miss the mark.

Ironically, I've found that the people who have the clearest and strongest sense of purpose have the most difficulty saying no to opportunities. Such leaders can justify how everything (or almost everything) can be related to

> **Ironically, I've found that the people who have the clearest and strongest sense of purpose have the most difficulty saying no to opportunities.**

what's most important to them. They believe every opportunity can have a positive impact on people, and thus, fulfill their purpose, so they dive in. I see this phenomenon most often in the leaders of nonprofit organizations and churches. They begin with a clear purpose, but they want to help everybody in every way, so they say yes far too often. After a couple of years, their staff members are exhausted and have scattered priorities. All of the activities met people's needs, but they weren't all included in the organization's central calling. Businesses usually aren't quite as eager to embrace every new idea and goal, but they also have difficulty staying on the main task.

In a book describing their business philosophy and experience in building companies, *A Better Way*, entrepreneurs Randy Keene and Tim McKibben address the necessity of being focused on the right things. They write,

> "Presidents [of companies] often make one of two glaring mistakes: they believe the purpose of the company is to make money, or they believe every good idea is worth pursuing. [We] realized profit is the byproduct of great people doing great work for a great purpose, but not every creative idea fits the company's necessarily narrow focus. When leaders invest people, time, and money in ventures that aren't central to the core business, they often redirect attention and efforts from the products and services that are most important. When this happens, they risk being spread too thin."[19]

Or as Stephen Covey famously wrote, "The main thing is to keep the main thing the main thing."[20]

We can even go back to the days of the Bible to see the importance of focus. The Apostle Paul wrote many of the letters we find in the New Testament. The historian Luke tells us how Paul's encounter with Christ on the road to Damascus turned his life upside down. He had been a ruthless persecutor of Christians, chasing them down, capturing them, imprisoning many and executing some. But he became the new champion of the cause. When Paul came to faith on the road to Damascus, there were only a handful of Christians in Palestine. Over the next three decades, he took the message of the gospel across the Roman Empire. In those years, he was attacked by Jews, misunderstood by Christians, beaten, stoned, and flogged in city after city. Through it all, this former persecutor had become a passionate, loving leader of the movement—in fact, he was one of the most effective entrepreneurs in the history of the world.

In a letter to the Christians in a city called Philippi, Paul explained his perspective on his purpose. His tenacity was now tempered by humility. He admitted his God-given purpose was all-consuming, and he hadn't yet fulfilled it completely. But instead of regretting his failures or lamenting the attacks he had suffered, he chose to look forward. He wrote:

> "Not that I have already obtained this or am already perfect, but I press on to make it my own, because Christ Jesus has made me his own. Brothers, I do not consider that I have made it my own. But one thing I do: forgetting what lies behind and straining forward to what lies ahead. I press on toward the goal for the prize of the upward call of God in Christ Jesus."[21]

"One thing I do." Paul had a compelling purpose that enabled him to maintain a clear priority. In spite of all the stress of leading the enterprise, and throughout his widely varied experiences of success, failure, adversity, and applause, he kept the main thing the main thing.

> **"One thing I do."**
>
> **—Paul**

FILTER

To get focused and remain focused, it's important to use your purpose as a filter as you consider all the goals, opportunities, and threats you face as a leader. It's like leaving a beloved dog in a kennel when you take a trip. When you return, you hear dozens of dogs barking, but only one is your dog. Every day in our offices, we hear dozens of dogs barking for our attention. Our job is to listen for our dog, the one that's our priority for that day, that team, that quarter, that season.

This metaphor, though, is incomplete because dog lovers probably aren't going to take more than one dog home from the kennel. In our companies, we may choose to open the doors and take more dogs home, but we need to make sure we keep them in the right order. If we let them all out at once, we experience chaos and a big mess! The job of a leader is to open the doors one at a time, in the right order, and communicate the sequence to all teams. Everyone then understands what they're doing, how each task relates to the purpose, and why they're doing the tasks in this order.

This isn't just an academic exercise. Pursuing the wrong priority or putting goals in the wrong order by failing to have a sole priority at any given time almost always results in failure to achieve our purpose.

What does this look like from a very practical point of view? Here's my recommendation:

1. As you plan your week, write your purpose statement at the top of a sheet of paper.

2. Make a list of the tasks, responsibilities, and opportunities for the week. This is your overall to-do list.

3. As you review the list, first mark the ones that are nonnegotiable; then of those, designate your top priority—if nothing else gets accomplished this week, this one must be done.

4. Mark those that are important but not crucial.

5. Mark those that scream for a yes but need a firm no.

6. And finally, assign each item that's still on the list to a day to be accomplished, and for each day, identify your priority.

7. Of course, you'll need to reevaluate your list and your priority first
   thing each morning (or the day before) to be sure you stay focused
   on the main thing each day.

For some of us, clarifying the priority is very easy. We intuitively
understand what's most important. This process is to make sure we
communicate both the *what* and the *why* to our teams.

But others are very detailed and careful in their analysis. They
weigh every option and consider pros and cons to the most minute
degree. It's okay for those leaders to take longer than their intuitive colleagues to come to the best conclusions, yet they need to avoid "analysis
paralysis." The people on their teams are waiting for direction, and the
leader needs to provide it. Not everything will be perfect. They'll make
mistakes, but those errors aren't the end of the world. They can learn
from missteps and make better choices next time. They, too, need to
communicate the what, the why, and the order of goals, but they don't
need to explain everything in minute detail. That takes too much time,
and there's a job for each person to do today!

When I gave the closing talk at a conference for organizational
consultants, I realized they had heard many inspiring and helpful messages over the three days of the event. I wanted to conclude by helping
them wade through all the good things to focus on the best. Before they
walked out the door and headed to the airport, I gave them this advice:

- Focus: Pick one good idea that you want to apply. You may have
  heard dozens, but pick one to work on when you get home.

- Deadline: Establish a timeline for when you want to accomplish it.
  A goal without a deadline is only a dream.

- Accountability: Tell someone about your goal and ask him or her
  to check in regularly to monitor your progress. Good intentions

often don't translate into reality unless someone comes along to encourage us, challenge us, and hold us accountable.

- Begin: Identify the very first step you'll take to accomplish your priority . . . and do it! It's easy to find excuses to put off getting started. (I found several excuses that sounded very reasonable when I needed to write that note to the person who had encouraged me.) The first step is often the hardest. If you can identify the priority and put a date on it, you're halfway there.

If leaders can consistently identify the priority for themselves and their teams—and link it to their stated purpose—they'll provide clarity, motivation, and direction for everyone involved. When the team is working on a major project or product, agreeing on the order of tasks reduces confusion and enhances productivity. It takes time and practice to consistently identify a team's priority and sequence its tasks, but before long, the leader gains confidence and the team becomes more effective. Looking at our priority through a clearer lens allows an individual, a team, and an organization to intentionally rise to a higher level of effectiveness.

Without having a priority to set the agenda, even a beautifully written purpose can seem disengaged, superfluous, and pointless.

Action expresses priorities.
— Mahatma Ghandi

TAKE A LOOK . . .

1. Does the idea of the singularity of priority (instead of *priorities*) make sense to you? Why or why not?

2. What's the connection between purpose and priority?

3. What are some practical ways you can "get rid of stupid" as you address competing goals?

4. Why do leaders often have far too many priorities? What are some of the consequences?

5. Why is the proper order in regard to each priority so important?

6. How might you change your weekly and daily planning to make sure you focus on your priority?

7. What's your first step?

CHAPTER 3
PEOPLE

The way you see people is the way you treat them,
and the way you treat them is what they become.
—*Johann Wolfgang von Goethe*

P olice officers have one of the most difficult jobs in the world. They often deal with people whose lives are twisted by drugs, poverty, and despair. I heard a touching story about an officer who patrolled a gang-infested section of a major city. Someone remarked to him, "I bet you have to deal with some really rough people."

He responded, "Actually, most of the time, I deal with good people on their worst day."

Wow. His answer challenges me to reconsider how I view the people I encounter each day. How do I see people? Do I believe the annoying people, the slow people, the critical people, the disengaged people that I'm interacting with are really "good people" who are just having a bad day? Or do I feel completely justified in writing them off with the labels I just used? I'm sure the officer's perspective of the human race shapes his interactions with every person he meets—those who are kind and compliant as well as those who are angry and defiant.

When we think about how we perceive people, many of us naturally see others in a binary way: as either good or bad. This chapter is about shifting that perspective, not from one to another, but by using a new lens to notice the complexity of each human being.

Labels matter. They become the headlines of the stories we tell ourselves about the people around us. "She's always negative." "He's incompetent." "She's naïve." "He's self-absorbed." "She's manipulative." "He's a liar." Labels are sticky—a few words become riveted in our minds and color every thought about a person and every interaction with him or her.

The way we see people affects how we treat them, and the way we treat them shapes how they see themselves and how they perform their roles in an organization. It's not rocket science: a person who feels valued is motivated to work hard, be creative, and find ways to help the team succeed. Conversely, a person who feels "less than" spends more time trying to read the leader's mind, defend turf, and jockey for position than supporting others on the team and accomplishing delegated tasks. Our perception of people, and the environment we create with them, makes coming to work a joy or a pain . . . for everybody.

Many people perceive others only by their surface level actions and attitudes, but leaders learn to see them for their true worth and value.

In the Introduction I told a story about the owner of a grocery store who was discouraged about the performance of his employees. He complained they weren't motivated, personable, or efficient, and he said his turnover rate was sky high. When I asked him about his hiring practices, he told me, "If people can tie their shoes and utter a complete sentence, I'll give them a job." How do you think his perception of his employees affected how he related to them? And how do you suppose his communication with them influenced their attitudes and performance? It's not hard to understand why their performance wasn't exemplary.

When people annoy or frustrate us, what if we tried to imagine something that may have prompted their behavior? For instance, what if:

- A guy cuts you off in traffic . . . because he just found out his child is sick and he's trying to get home as fast as possible.

- A snarky woman screams at your customer service reps . . . because she was recently divorced and hasn't processed all the hurt, fear, and new feelings of abandonment.

- A person on your team is late to work three days in a row . . . because his mom left home again and he has to drive a long way to take his younger brother to school.

- A young man in the office is increasingly forgetful and unfocused . . . because his wife just had their third child and neither of them is getting much sleep.

- A client suddenly becomes unresponsive and then uncooperative . . . because her husband just lost his job.

- An older man is grouchy and sullen . . . because his wife was just diagnosed with dementia, and he's terrified of the future.

Some of you reading this right now are rolling your eyes. You and I both know that most of these scenarios are contrived. I agree, most of them *may not* be true most of the time, but they *could be* once in a while. And in case they are, I want to err on the side of caution. The point is that we are usually much too quick to judge the actions of people without even considering what might be behind some of those actions. Why are we so reluctant to give people the benefit of the doubt even though we know how great it feels when they do it for us?

There can be a myriad of reasons why good people sometimes have a bad day. If we jump to the conclusion that a less than brilliant performance or attitude is a character flaw, our response will almost certainly be short, demanding, and critical. Our challenge is to give people the benefit of the doubt . . . at least once, maybe two or three times. After that, we probably need to ask what's going on. At that point, we'll do one of three things:

1. We discover the source, and our compassion will go even deeper;

2. We realize the person has a chronic problem and we adjust expectations or make a change; or

3. If it's solvable, we can address the problem with kindness, strength, and clarity.

Jumping to conclusions prevents the opportunity of identifying the real problem and finding a workable resolution . . . and it almost always causes the other person to become defensive.

IN A BOX

I've been part of a company where I didn't feel valued. What's really odd is that I was one of the founders of the company, but after we invited another person to join our leadership team, my experience soon began to turn sour. The new guy's messages, spoken and unspoken, made it clear that he was there to churn out profits, and I was just a cog in his machine. My role was to promote our company's value to prospective clients and communicate our vision and strategy to our team. The leader let me do my thing, but it was obvious he believed his role was more central to the company's life and growth, and my role was little more than window dressing. Quite often, when he was in the room as I shared my heart with the team, he gave me a look like a teacher would give to a student who had tried really hard but didn't do very well at all. I felt patronized, overlooked, undervalued. I was sure he saw me as "Kevin, the windup monkey whose sole purpose is to entertain the crowd."

We hired people to join our team, but this leader saw himself as more important than any of us. He didn't have to say, "I'm the most important" or "I have the most valuable experience" because we all sensed that was his perspective. When people don't feel honored and valued, they instinctively try to prove themselves, please the one who has power, or hide to escape criticism. His condescending tone created competition among several team members to get his attention. We were more interested in winning applause and protecting our turf than helping each other succeed. Even though my sense of purpose was clear and strong, I didn't know where I fit, and I had difficulty navigating the relational landmines among our team members.

This guy pigeon-holed me as an unessential standup communicator, and for a while, I believed that was all I could contribute to the organization—I bought what he was selling about me. When I eventually got out from under his limiting leadership, I discovered I possessed untapped managerial abilities to do things he would never have dreamed of letting me do.

When people put us in a box, we tend to stay in it for a long time. And when we put others in boxes, they stay there, too. If we label the boxes "Talented," "Valuable," "Essential," "Competent," "Kind," and "Thoughtful," people will almost certainly live up to those evaluations. But if we use labels like "one-trick pony," "too much trouble," "untrustworthy," or "a pain in the butt," we create resentment, defiance, a desperation to please, competition for accolades, a desire to withdraw from any threat of condemnation, or other problems. The labels become self-fulfilling because the way leaders see their people becomes how they see themselves, which then prompts them to act out the roles they've been assigned.

LIFE AND DEATH

The power of words can cut both ways. A few years ago, a former star pitcher from Major League Baseball gave a talk at a maximum-security prison for Bill Glass Ministries. The athlete wanted to explain how God sees his children as loved and valuable, even when they are flawed. To illustrate his point, he told the men about playing catch with his father in their backyard. When he was a little boy and just learning to throw the ball, he sometimes threw it over his father's head. Instead of getting angry and criticizing him, his dad affirmed him, "You've really got a gun for an arm, son! Way to go! You're going to be a major league pitcher one day!"

After his talk, a prisoner who was serving a life sentence came up to him and said, "When I was a kid, my dad always told me I wouldn't amount to anything and I'd end up in prison. I guess both of our dads were right." The Bible says, "Death and life are in the power of the tongue."[22] This brief interaction demonstrates both results.

> We need to avoid the words "always" and "never."

Being positive and affirming doesn't mean we become blind. I'm not suggesting leaders gather their teams and sit around a campfire sharing only happy stories. Good leaders see the reality in others' lives and point out what needs to be changed, but they offer hope for a better future instead of demanding change and threatening condemnation. We need to avoid the words "always" and "never." Such absolutes reinforce the hopelessness of change and prompt us to keep using destructive labels. Instead, we need to maintain a clear-eyed view of people's attitudes and behavior. If we see them as good and valuable, we'll treat them with respect . . . and that often makes all the difference in the world. Like the policeman, we will realize we're encountering good people on their bad days.

Of course, if underperforming people fail to respond to our honesty, hope, and a path forward, we need to make changes for the sake of the team and the purpose of the organization. But I believe most people are hungry for hope; they thirst for affirmation. If we replace negative labels with positive ones, and communicate the new narrative clearly and frequently, the vast majority of people will make major strides forward. I've seen it too often to doubt.

FEELING COMPLETELY JUSTIFIED

I have my own struggles with trying to avoid labeling people. One of my old friends I've labeled as "hopelessly cynical." Whenever she comes to mind, that's the term that flashes in my head. I may be convinced that I have every right to view her that way, but such a perception diminishes her value to me. It may not create a shift from "friend" to "enemy," but I shouldn't even think of her as an annoyance.

Negative labels give us a sense of power over others. We feel superior when we deem other people inferior. We tell ourselves, "I'd never act that way," or "I'd never treat anyone like that." I'm quick to correct others who label people, but for some reason, I feel completely justified in doing it myself. I've become skilled at misdirecting my critiques so I appear to be innocent, yet I get the point across. I might say, "I know she means well, but . . ." or "I hate to say anything, but you need to know this about that person," or "We all know what's going on with him." While avoiding direct criticism, such comments give me cover to say anything I want to say about someone.

As leaders, we're in positions to do enormous good or inflict enormous harm . . . and anything in between. We need to take stock of our relationships at home and at work. We should consider how we think others see us and then take a look at how we view them.

As leaders, we're in positions to do enormous good or inflict enormous harm . . . and anything in between.

First, we might ask ourselves some hard questions about how we see others:

- Do we feel threatened by their exceptional talents?

- Do we feel afraid of their intimidation?

- Do we feel used and manipulated for their gain?

- Do we feel ignored or taken for granted?

- Do we feel valued, honored, and respected?

And then, we can ask some questions about how they perceive us:

- Do they think we're trying to use our talents to wield power over them?

- Do they assume we're only satisfied when we dominate and they cower?

- Do they think we're using them as stepping-stones to reach our goals?

- Do they believe we overlook people who aren't performing up to our standards or who annoy us?

- Do the people on our teams believe we're glad to have them around?

These aren't easy questions to answer, and we shouldn't rush through them too quickly. If we're thorough and honest, they force us to reach beyond our habits and natural inclinations to examine what's in our hearts. How we view ourselves determines how we see others, and how we see them determines how we treat them. Quite often, the first problem to be solved isn't them . . . it's us.

I'm afraid many people in our organizations have a mistaken view of what it means to be kind to others. Some of them assume being kind means never saying anything corrective. Author Tim Keller explains that our communication needs a strong blend of love and truth. He is writing about communication in marriage, but the principle applies in every significant relationship: "Love without truth is sentimentality; it supports and affirms us but keeps us in denial about our flaws. Truth without love is harshness; it gives information but in such a way that we cannot really hear it."[23]

In another lesson on the nature of kindness, Keller uses three of the five sisters in Jane Austen's *Pride and Prejudice* (Jane, Mary, and Lizzy) to illustrate different approaches and outcomes. Even if you haven't read the book or seen the movie, you'll instantly recognize the three types of kindness.

Jane, the oldest sister, is "temperamentally pleasant." She has a naturally good-natured disposition. She always sees the best in everyone and every situation, so we can't imagine her speaking a corrective word to anyone.

Mary, the third sister, is "manipulatively nice." The book's narrator reveals Mary's motive: "Mary, who having, in consequence of being the only plain one in the family [the most unattractive of all the women], worked hard for knowledge and accomplishments, was always impatient for display. . . . [Vanity] had given her likewise a pedantic air and conceited manner."

Keller explains the narrator's point:

"Jane Austen says whenever Mary is talking to people about Christian truth and Christian loyalty, trying to tell her sisters how to be good people, why is she doing it? Why? What's the heart? It's not about truth. It's not about honesty. It's not about Christianity. It's not about God, and it's not even about her sisters. It's about her. She feels inadequate."[24]

Mary acts nice (and desperately tries to be good and knowledgeable and right) to win approval. She can't be content unless people are impressed with her generosity, and Jane can't be content unless everyone around her is happy. But Lizzy exemplifies a third category.

For much of the story, Lizzy is harsh and sarcastic toward Mr. Darcy, a wealthy but aloof gentleman she has met. Her demeanor is quite prejudiced in response to the seemingly prideful Darcy, a trait which gives the book its title. However, in the course of the story, Lizzy's heart is melted by Darcy's love. By the end, her natural inclination to be critical has been transformed into genuine kindness. She is still observant and insightful about people, but those traits are no longer motivated by suspicion and prejudice—they are shaped and empowered by love.[25]

I'm pretty sure most people would say I'm temperamentally nice. They mean it as a compliment (I hope), but I want to move toward Lizzy's form of kindness. Most of us can easily spot people who are manipulatively nice. Their syrupy insincerity and self-righteousness is hard to swallow. In relationships that matter—at home, with friends, and at work—we need to identify where we are on the "niceness scale," and make adjustments to become more like Lizzy . . . at least Lizzy at the end of the book!

PEOPLE TO AVOID

Experts identify several types of leaders. Some are like military generals barking commands to the troops; some try to build consensus so everyone is on board; some lead the charge and assume others will follow; some cast a powerful vision that inspires commitment; and others are coaches who are deeply involved in developing their people. I see myself as a blend of visionary and coach. One of my strengths is that I try to see the best in people, but the corresponding leadership deficit is that I can often be (let me try to say this gently) a bit naïve, a tad gullible, and slow to realize that some people aren't giving their best.

As an expert in business management, John W. Gardner warns us: "Pity the leader caught between unloving critics and uncritical lovers." In other words, leaders need more than a dash of shrewdness in all our relationships. If we're not careful, unloving critics will crush our enthusiasm, darken our vision, and leave us preoccupied with attempts to manage the malcontents. Uncritical admirers seem harmless enough, but their unvarnished and unwavering praise isn't what we need. Let's take a closer look at these two extremes.

If you're charting a new path for your company or your team, creating a new product, offering new services, or taking any kind of significant risk, you're sure to hear the roar of the critics. They lie quietly for a while, but when they start to see change, they rise up and jeer. They insist your idea is dumb and your strategy is stupid. They are unloving opponents: they don't care about you or your organization (although they may hold prominent positions). They're more interested in being seen and heard—and being right—than offering constructive analysis and feedback.

For a long time, I was shocked when I encountered such people. My purpose is "To inspire people today to impact tomorrow," but many people outside our organization were absolutely sure no "real" businesses would care about our purpose and our strategies. Again and again, they delighted in scoffing at me and our message. The problem was that I took their criticism to heart far too much. Of course, I need to listen to constructive feedback, but this wasn't constructive. It was meant to deflate, to demean, and to diminish our impact. It took me a while to stop caring so much about what those people thought and said, but I finally was able to take off the blinders and see clearly what they were doing.

I also find plenty of people in Gardner's other category: uncritical lovers. Instead of being overly critical and cynical (blind to the good), these people are unflinchingly positive (blind to the flaws). They want to be on the inside, to feel like they're part of the team, so they tell us what they assume we want to hear. Certainly, all of us want to be affirmed and encouraged, but blind allegiance isn't true allegiance. What is the goal of these fawning sycophants? I think they want to be close to those who are powerful and attractive . . . close enough to be included with them in some way, but not honest enough to speak the truth when it's necessary. Oprah Winfrey has seen her share of uncritical lovers. She commented, "Everyone wants to ride with you in the limo, but what you want is someone who will take the bus with you when the limo breaks down."

When we hear only the uncritical lovers, we'll confidently stride directly into failure.

We can't trust the words of people who can't be truthful and objective. Leaders need to be secure enough to listen to honest critiques and avoid the lure of the echo chamber filled with people who only tell us how great we are. If we value only praise, we probably won't be able to hear those who tell us the often complex and sometimes hard truth. When we hear only the uncritical lovers, we'll confidently stride directly into failure, leaving us surprised and confused. Gardner's quote continues: "Leaders need reassurance, but just as important they need advisors who tell them the truth, gently but candidly."[26]

Neither unloving critics nor uncritical lovers take us where we need to go. In very different ways, they both stunt our growth. We desperately need to recruit people in a third category: loving critics. With open eyes and good hearts, they tell us the truth: the affirming truth when they see we've done something good, and the corrective truth when we're sliding off track. Surround yourself with these people. Treasure them, listen to them, and learn from them.

We also need to be loving critics to the people around us. They don't need harsh criticism, and they don't benefit from syrupy sweetness. I'm learning the value of saying hard things to the people I care about. It's not easy for me, but it's necessary. *Wall Street Journal* columnist Peggy Noonan offers this insight: "Candor is a compliment; it implies equality. It's how true friends talk."[27] I want to have this kind of friend, and I want to be this kind of friend . . . and this kind of leader.

THE LAW OF ORGANIZATIONAL GROWTH

Sometimes, the tension on a team isn't the result of one bad day or an error of miscommunication; it's that the person isn't a good fit—and leaders often put up with the mismatch far too long. From time to time I've heard business leaders say, "When I fire someone, I'm freeing him up for a better future." I've always thought that was a glib (and perhaps heartless) statement, but I'm beginning to see the wisdom in it.

When a person doesn't prove himself or herself and contribute to the success of the team after plenty of training and opportunities, it's time to make a change. Firing such people not only eliminates one of the biggest headaches for leaders; it's also essential to the culture of the team, the performance of the company, and yes, even the person's future. Remaining stuck in a job he or she can't do certainly won't build the person's self-esteem and enhance skills! Letting those people stay may prevent an awkward conversation, but it continues to absorb the leader's time and energy, sends a message to the team that mediocrity (or worse) is acceptable, and keeps the person from seeing the truth that he or she simply doesn't fit in that kind of role.

As I interact with leaders in businesses and nonprofits, they tell me the number one issue they face is the struggle to hire the best people. If I have time to go deeper into conversations with them, they often explain that they want to find people who will fill the holes in their organizations. In most cases, they're looking for someone who will prove to be better than the people they currently have on their team. That makes perfect sense, but there's a paradox. People who are new to a team typically rise or fall to the level of the existing culture. To put it simply, we tend to reproduce what we have, not what we want.

To put it simply, we tend to reproduce what we have, not what we want.

A study by the Kenan-Flagler Business School at the University of North Carolina asked millennials what they are looking for in their employment. Sixty-five percent of those polled expressed the desire to find a job that promotes their personal development.[28] That's great news for employers! It dispels the myth that most millennials entering the workforce only want to collect a paycheck. The truth is that they're willing to contribute—they just want to be challenged, to learn, and to acquire skills that will propel them in their careers.

When Google executives analyzed their hiring practices and effectiveness in a study called "Project Oxygen," they came to a startling conclusion. They had assumed they needed to focus on students who were graduating with a strong proficiency in the STEM subjects: science, technology, engineering, and math. Founders Sergey Brin and Larry Page set their algorithms to select the top students in those fields, but when they analyzed the data that showed the qualities necessary for their employees, STEM expertise came in last on the list. Instead, "The seven top characteristics of success at Google are all soft skills: being a good coach; communicating and listening well; possessing insights into others (including others' different values and points of view); having empathy toward and being supportive of one's colleagues; being a good critical thinker and problem solver; and being able to make connections across complex ideas."

A second study, "Project Aristotle," was conducted more recently and reinforced the previous results: "The best teams at Google exhibit a range of soft skills: equality, generosity, curiosity toward the ideas of your teammates, empathy, and emotional intelligence. And topping the list: emotional safety. No bullying. To succeed, each and every team member must feel confident speaking up and making mistakes. They must know they are being heard."

In the *Washington Post* article describing these studies, author Valerie Strauss concludes, "Broad learning skills are the key to long-term, satisfying, productive careers. What helps you thrive in a changing world isn't rocket science. It may just well be social science, and, yes, even the humanities and the arts that contribute to making you not just workforce ready but *world* ready."[29]

But hiring new employees is a grueling task, and virtually all of us have stories of hiring disasters. In smaller companies, and sometimes even in large ones, executives soon tire of the tedium of reviewing résumés, holding interviews, and wading through the options. Too often, those leaders delegate this crucial task to someone else. If that "someone else" is highly skilled and passionate, things may go well, but exhausted executives sometimes delegate hiring to someone who doesn't exhibit the qualities they want in new employees. When eager, young millennials are looking for a culture that values passion and excellence, they won't be attracted to a company whose first foot forward is anything less.

When pastor Andy Stanley gives dating advice, he tells people, "Become the person that the person you're looking for is looking for." I love that thought. If you really want to attract the right person, you need to become what the other person desires. It's the exact same principle in hiring: if we create a team with a dynamic, effective culture we'll attract dynamic, effective people to join us.

People who are not talented, creative, and enthusiastic aren't likely to attract others who are.

There's nothing wrong with wanting to hire the best talent, but we probably won't attract people who are more qualified than the people already on our teams. We need to create an environment that top-tier applicants would dream to be part of. The priority, then, is to develop your existing team first, and they will then attract the kind of people you want to hire. People who are not talented, creative, and enthusiastic aren't likely to attract others who are.

After we find someone who is a good fit for a team, we then need to put that person in a position to succeed. Far too often, a passive corporate culture rewards people for only taking up space. And sometimes the established systems of reporting, permissions, and rigid rules actually inhibit people from doing great work. Individuals who don't rock the boat are rewarded, and those who show initiative are suspect.

I heard one manager comment about a particularly gifted person who showed a lot of promise: "I'd like to promote her, but I can't because she hasn't been here long enough." This is just one evidence of a dysfunctional system. As leaders, we need to minimize the red tape and reward initiative. Only then can we get the right people in the right place and give them the right tools to accomplish the right priority. Rewards for excellent work aren't always a corner office and financial perks. We can reward people in countless ways, starting with giving them the credit they deserve and thanking them publicly. We also reward them by asking for their input on problems that might be out of their normal range of responsibilities. When we broaden their influence, we tell them and the rest of the team that impact means more than rigid adherence to the limits of a job description.

At various points in our leadership, all of us will hit a wall with someone. No matter how hard we try, we can't seem to make things work out. Such conflicts are very draining for me. Some time ago, I was in a business relationship that I was sure was going to be great for both of us. Gradually, the luster of the first weeks and months wore off. I assumed our difficulties were misunderstandings, so I doubled my efforts to communicate often and clearly. It didn't help. I found myself thinking far more about managing this relationship—and frankly, protecting myself from the other person's behavior—than advancing the business. We finally came to a point where it was obvious our connection couldn't move forward . . . and the inevitable separation cost a lot of money. I felt very discouraged. I wasn't used to failing in relationships. And if I'm honest, my disappointment had more than its share of resentment, and I was moving into full-blown bitterness.

At a low point, I had a conversation with David Salyers, a Vice President of Marketing for Chick-fil-A. David advised me to look at the situation from a very different angle. Instead of seeing it as a personal failure and a financial setback, he suggested I see the time and money I'd lost as the best learning experience I could possibly receive. With a knowing smile, David said, "Kevin, I challenge you to change your perspective on all that has happened. You need to see what happened as if you attended the best school you could imagine. When people get an MBA, it costs them time and money, but they don't look at it as a loss, they see it as an investment. Your difficult experience is like earning an MBA. You've paid money and spent time to learn a very valuable lesson—one you'll remember the rest of your life." It was great advice. With some difficulty because my emotions were still raw, I began to see all the heartache as time and money *invested* instead of time and money *wasted*. This new lens has made a lot of difference in my mood and thoughts. I'm no longer as preoccupied with all the "what ifs" and "if onlys." I'm not quite thankful yet for what happened, but at least I can see some real wisdom I've gained from the experience.

Years ago, I heard someone say that when we despise someone, our world gets smaller. We try to avoid that person, and our resentment makes us self-absorbed—we can't stop thinking about the person, what happened, and what we've lost. I don't want my world to shrink, so I'm thankful David helped me find a different perspective on this very painful situation. With his encouragement, I'm looking toward a hopeful future instead of back at the painful past.

We may not have a lot of these very difficult relationships, but it doesn't take many to consume our minds and hearts for long seasons of time. Far more often, conflicts can be resolved and misunderstandings rectified so the person and the team can move forward.

BE A TAILOR

How do we develop the people on our teams? Like every other aspect of leadership, we need to see the opportunities and the process more clearly. I heard a college football coach talking about how he was handling a freshman who was the starting quarterback for his team. The freshman didn't have years of practice and game experience to help familiarize himself with

It's easier to tailor the game plan for the player than try to tailor the player for the game plan.

the complexities of the college team's offense. The coach explained his leadership philosophy: "We're creating plays for our quarterback." He didn't have unrealistic expectations of the young man. The coach realized it's easier to tailor the game plan for the player than try to tailor the player for the game plan. Instead of "I have a system and you need to fit into it," this wise coach concluded, "I'll change the system so you—and the team—will have the best shot at winning."

Many companies and other organizations use temperament assessment tools to help them understand their current team members and hire new members who have the best chance of fitting in. These assessments—DiSC, Myers-Briggs, Kolbe Index, or any others—help us lead like the football coach: we can more fully understand the strengths and limitations various individuals bring to our teams. When we grasp their temperament and communication styles, we can tailor our communication (and our expectations) so we lead each person most effectively. We may use consultants to help our teams process the information we gain from the assessments, or we may just dive in to discuss what we've learned about ourselves and each other. This isn't wasted time. It's essential to enable us to tap into each person's motivational style, bring out the best performance, and create a culture that attracts the best people.

Yes, I realize some people have used the results of these assessments as excuses that they can't change and need to be handled in a particular way—a defensive stance that undermines the usefulness of the tool and disregards the power of our differences to make us all stronger and wiser. Good leaders use these tools to promote mutual understanding, but also to encourage, correct, and direct individuals on their teams so each one feels valued and empowered to excel. The most gifted leaders take time to understand how their communication is heard, not just what is said, and they interact in ways that are most effective for their people.

Our understanding of each person's communication style, temperament, and skills helps us avoid derogatory labels. We may have seen someone as annoying, but we begin to see her as analytical. We may have seen someone as slow, but now we see him as thorough. We have seen another person as impulsive, but we begin to value her creativity. A different lens enables us to see strengths where we saw only flaws, and this perception revolutionizes our relationships and our team's performance.

But understanding can have a downside. In the past, I've been too positive, too willing to let something slide without confronting the person, and too slow to say anything that will make people uncomfortable. Usually, sensitivity and kindness provide a very positive atmosphere for people, but I have difficulty saying hard things, and my reluctance has had a negative impact on our team. When I don't address obvious problems, and when I allow someone to remain on the team who really needs to go, I'm admitting that my comfort is more important than the health of our team's culture.

I've had to realize that when I value my comfort over truth, I erode trust on our team. Candor isn't a bad thing. In fact, one of the most important characteristics of a good leader is the willingness to speak the truth . . . sometimes glorious and affirming truth, but other times hard and painful truth. Honesty combined with kindness is fertile ground for each person's development and the team's ability to flourish.

> **I've had to realize that when I value my comfort over truth, I erode trust on our team.**

Our view of people extends to our relationships with vendors, customers, and clients. If we have a sour view that those people exist only to make our lives harder, they certainly will. But if we see them as valuable allies whose lives are complex, and who need us to play a small role in making their lives better, we'll treat them with great respect. One of the things that drives me crazy is when I'm waiting, often at the airport, and the person at the counter doesn't even acknowledge the existence of people in the line. To that disconnected agent, people are little more than impersonal numbers. But I've also seen plenty of agents give eye contact, smile, and treat people the way the agents want to be treated. The Golden Rule is considered precious for a reason.

I heard a leader make a startling statement. He said that every time he picks up the phone, has an appointment, or walks into a meeting, he reminds himself, "I am now going to talk to a person created by God and of incalculable worth." He said that simple, profound reminder has revolutionized his connection with every person in his life. If we believe everyone has great value, we'll treat them with both candor and kindness. Candor without kindness may be true, but it's hard to hear. Kindness without candor is trite and mushy. The blend of candor and kindness enables us to live in the truth. We can then communicate with people in a way they're more likely to hear both affirmation and correction. When we look at people through this lens, we're less defensive and demanding, and we're more patient and honest.

As leaders, we need to periodically check our lenses to see if they're clear or if they've become clouded by cynicism about others or doubt about ourselves. When we see others as "good people" even on their worst days, we provide a powerful environment in which people can grow and excel.

> *Leadership is about making others better as a result of your presence,*
> *making sure that impact lasts in your absence.*
> —*Sheryl Sandberg*

TAKE A LOOK . . .

1. Do you believe the people who are the most difficult to lead are really "good people on their worst days"? Explain your answer.

2.   Have you ever been on a team when you didn't feel valued by your leader? How did he or she communicate this message? How did it affect you? How did you respond?

3.   Describe the most positive relationship you've had with a leader.

4.   What are some ways you can determine if you are "temperamentally pleasant," "manipulatively nice," "genuinely kind," or maybe don't even bother trying to be sweet, nice, or kind at all? How might identifying where you currently fall on this list help you move toward communicating with authentic kindness and truth?

5. The "law of organizational growth" says that we reproduce what we have, not what we want. How have you seen this principle played out in an organization? How is it currently being demonstrated in *your* organization?

6. What are some ways you can tailor your leadership to maximize the potential of everyone you work with?

7. How would it affect your perception of people if, before every conversation or meeting, you reminded yourself, "I am now going to talk to a person created by God and of incalculable worth"?

CHAPTER 4

PROCESS

Efficiency is doing things right; effectiveness is doing the right things.
—Peter Drucker

An organization's "process" is the way tasks and people are organized to get the job done. It includes established rules, regulations, planning, reporting, evaluating, and quality assurance. I place a high value on spontaneity and flexibility, so whenever I read an article or hear speakers talk about the necessity of implementing a process in their businesses, I cringe. It's not me—I resist being bound by processes.

The Kolbe A Index leadership assessment evaluates several traits of effective leaders. Not surprisingly, I rated high in what they call "quick start," but I was on the other end of the spectrum for "fact finding" and "follow-through." The report confirmed what I already knew to be true: I'm energized to start things, and I love working with people, but I despise the grind of working through a myriad of details.

Other leaders are the polar opposite: they have difficulty starting new projects, but after a project gets going, they invest plenty of time in research and feel completely comfortable moving methodically to accomplish their goal. They feel more confident when things are clearly spelled out and they have plenty of time to work the system. The staff at Kolbe would say I'm "resistant" to process, the people on the other end of the spectrum are "insistent" on process, and those in the middle are "adaptable" to process.[30]

Some people use *systems* as a synonym for *process*. Even the word *system* seems stifling to me, although I realize systems are necessary if

I want our company to excel in anything we do. I have come to understand that a workable process is what provides repeatable success. Some people implement processes intuitively; I have to be very intentional about them.

The purpose sets the direction, the priority establishes the order we do them, and getting the right people in the right places to solve the right problems is crucial, but then it's also necessary for leaders to implement workable (and I'd insist, flexible) systems so the team can work smoothly and effectively. I may hate the idea of processes, but I know they're necessary. My team needs them, our customers and clients need them, our partners need them, and yes, I have to admit, I need them. Process provides consistency, and consistency provides a platform to replicate peak performance. All leaders come to their roles with a particular perspective about process. The best of us realize we need to see this vital leadership trait more clearly so we can make necessary adjustments.

Many people perceive all processes to be either unimportant or of paramount importance, but astute leaders learn to see how the right process enables a team to reproduce success.

I wrote *8 Essential Exchanges* to clarify the choices we need to make between things that seem *good* and those that are *better*. One of the choices I encourage people to make is to exchange expedience for excellence. At a conference where I spoke on this topic, I waxed eloquent about the importance of pursuing excellence. After I finished, a man introduced himself and asked, "Kevin, how would you define excellence?"

In my response, I repeated some of what I'd said in my talk about the difference between expedience (cutting corners to get quick results) and excellence (pursuing the best), but I realized I didn't have a good, crisp description of what it means to pursue the best. It looks somewhat different in different settings, and I realized I should have a better answer than I gave him at that moment.

After that conversation, I read an interview with George Brett, one of the greatest hitters in the history of Major League Baseball. He played his entire career with the Kansas City Royals. He was one of only four players in the history of the game to amass over 3000 hits, 300 home runs, and a career .300 batting average. He was elected to the Hall of Fame in a landslide vote in 1999. Near the end of his last season in 1993, a reporter asked him, "How do you want your last play in your last game to go?"

I'm sure the reporter assumed Brett would paint a dramatic picture of hitting a game-winning grand slam in the bottom of the ninth inning of the last game of the World Series, but that's not what he said. He had obviously thought about that moment because he responded without hesitation: "I'd like my last play in baseball to go something like this: I'll hit a slow, routine groundball to the second baseman. He'll field it cleanly and throw me out at first, but it'll be close because I'm running as hard as I can to get to the bag. I want it to always be said that George Brett gave his best and tried his hardest until the end. I want people to say, 'He left it all on the field, not just in the dramatic moments, but all the time.' I don't think I can play any other way but all out. I enjoy the game so much because I'm putting so much into it." That was George Brett's concept of his pursuit of excellence, and I haven't found anything better. For him and for us, excellence never "just happens." It's the result of an intentional process, rigorously pursued and patiently followed.

Organizational excellence isn't revealed only in customer service awards, million-dollar contracts, newly-released software sensations, or being featured in a cover article in *Forbes*. Those may be some of the end results, but a commitment to excellence can also be seen in ordinary events and mundane moments. Good leaders recognize their team members' passion to do a great job even if there is no fanfare, and in fact, even if no one else notices.

> **Good leaders recognize their team members' passion to do a great job even if there is no fanfare, and in fact, even if no one else notices.**

ALL KINDS

Process feels constricting to people like me, yet repeatable and workable systems are the platform for producing replicable results—for individuals as they contribute their best, for the team as their synergy produces exemplary products and services, and for the customer who sees the results of the team's commitment to excellence. Without a good process, success is difficult to achieve . . . and nearly impossible to repeat.

Some of us are very intuitive leaders. We create systems just good enough to get by, but when those systems cease to be productive, we can't say why . . . and we don't know how to fix them. A new lens, a fresh perspective, is needed to see the value in going beyond intuition to craft a process that works today, will work tomorrow, and works for every member of the team. I may have to push myself to make this happen, but I know I will benefit in the long run, and you will too.

From clear empirical evidence, I've discovered that my perspective on process drives my wife crazy. Laura is a disciplined, dedicated person who has very clear goals and follows all the rules to achieve them. She graduated from college without making a B. I could almost say the same thing, but I was often on the bottom side, looking up at Bs. She went on to graduate school to become a physician's assistant. She lives by the book, and she's been very successful.

My style is a little different: I'm not sure where the book is, and if I found it, I probably wouldn't even read it. I sense what's going on, and I process information quickly to reach a conclusion. Laura might come to the same conclusion, but she would take much longer because she gathers facts and sorts through the options. My disdain for process annoys her. She can't imagine how my way of making decisions can possibly work. Thankfully, I'm not alone. One of my good friends is Dr. Grant Zarzour. Grant loves to create new things and challenge the status quo. One of his mantras is: "The rules don't apply to leaders." His point is that people who shake things up, who move people forward, and who ultimately change the world often live outside the box of normal rules and processes. It's not that rules aren't valuable, but we may not innovate if we don't play outside of the lines.

Sometimes those who think outside the box and defy prescribed rules find entirely new ways to accomplish their goals. For most of recorded history, track athletes who starred in the high jump went over the bar in the same way: kicking their legs up and rolling over the bar face down. But Dick Fosbury tried a new technique in the 1968 Summer Olympics in Mexico City. At first, people laughed at his approach of going over the bar facing up, with his head and shoulders crossing the bar before his torso and legs. But then they realized Fosbury was jumping higher than anyone had ever jumped before! In fact, he won the gold medal at the games. The Fosbury Flop became a sensation in the world of track and field, and it's still being used. Dick Fosbury didn't let the accepted process limit his imagination. He saw something different, something better, something that might look odd at first but that revolutionized his sport.

A disdain for rules carries with it a certain amount of risk. People like Grant and me, who thrive outside normal conventions, may accomplish great things, but we're also prone to crash and burn. I remember my father talking about my friend Travis when we were in high school. Everyone liked Travis, but he didn't usually follow the rules. After meeting Travis a few times, my dad commented, "That kid will either become a multi-millionaire or he'll end up in jail. I don't see many options in between!"

Other leaders, of course, are on the other end of the continuum. They seem to be more devoted to the systems than to the workers who use them or the people who ultimately benefit from them. Those leaders need to step back, analyze how to streamline their processes to eliminate busywork, and determine how they can make work more meaningful for each person on the team—especially those who may not value processes quite as much.

Thankfully, most leaders fall somewhere in between these poles. They instinctually sense what's working and what's holding people back, but they also realize processes are necessary to facilitate communication, clarify expectations, and get jobs done on time.

> **They instinctually sense what's working and what's holding people back, but they also realize processes are necessary to facilitate communication, clarify expectations, and get jobs done on time.**

Depending on the type of business, processes may need to be clear and established before you start production, or they might be perfected as you're rolling out a product. At times a leader's devotion to create a perfect process limits innovation; other times it is absolutely necessary to provide a platform before innovation will flourish. The process needed for an efficient dog grooming company will be radically different from one for Amazon, Microsoft, or NASA.

We need to remember two things: (1) in our bias about process, everyone falls somewhere on the spectrum of *resistant* to *adaptable* to *insistent*; and (2) if we don't acknowledge the bias and learn to appreciate the other point of view, we'll limit the effectiveness of our leadership, the performance of our teams, and the productivity of our organizations.

Personal bias isn't a character flaw . . . but it reveals one if we're not honest about it. Mark Miller is a leadership expert and author of several books. I picked up this illustration from him: When I speak at a conference, I will point to someone in the first row wearing glasses and ask him, "Excuse me, but why are you wearing glasses?"

After he gets over being put on the spot in front of his peers, he typically responds (almost sarcastically), "So I can see."

I then say, "So, what you're communicating to the world is that without your glasses, you wouldn't be able to see very well. Is that right?"

The person nods. The point seems to be self-evident to him and the hundreds of others who are eavesdropping on this very public conversation. I continue, "You have a weakness, and you're showcasing it to the world."

I then turn to the audience and ask, "Does anyone think this person is less of a leader because he's wearing glasses?" The headshaking and audible noes tell me they get the point, so I continue, "No, of course not. No one thinks this person is less of a leader because he's wearing glasses." I continue, "Want to know something crazy? Do you know that some people who don't even need glasses wear 'fake' ones because they think the glasses make them look smarter?"

To reinforce the point, I challenge them to remember that some of us are so afraid for anyone to know we have a weakness that we never want to admit it. However, when we acknowledge our weakness or bias and learn to compensate for it, people think more highly of us and respect our leadership even more.

I've realized the value of acknowledging my bias against process. Before I was upfront with our team, I didn't want to appear weak or deficient, but they already knew. When I was vulnerable enough to tell them the truth about myself, trust didn't erode. Trust was strengthened. Now, as I continue to acknowledge my bias, they give me more grace, and they're more eager to jump in to fill in the gaps I leave as our team creates and uses workable, repeatable systems.

When leaders accurately perceive their bias related to process (or any of the other leadership concepts I'm addressing in this book), they can hire to their weaknesses, invite input without being defensive, and gradually move toward the middle and becoming more adaptable.

In my interactions with leaders in different industries and organizations, it appears that most of them are on the insistent end of the scale. They prefer safety and predictability, and they only feel comfortable with limited creativity. Process-averse people who prefer to rely on intuition and don't seem to value facts and reason drive them crazy. If those very organized people don't recognize their bias and learn to appreciate the other viewpoint, they'll applaud only those who follow the rules, and they'll hire people just like themselves. Before long, the team may be very efficient, but the unspoken purpose becomes protecting the established process instead of focusing on the best ways to make things easy, better, and more effective. A rigid system soon becomes self-absorbed, self-promoting, and self-defeating.

In contrast, my encounters with entrepreneurs show that the vast majority of them think outside the box. They thrive on creativity and risk, not perfecting existing processes. They, too, need to acknowledge their bias and value people who can turn their crazy ideas into reality. If they don't find people who operate differently than they do, they'll never realize the full potential of their ideas.

I've observed that most organizations reward the status quo. They celebrate the efficiency of their systems and work hard to make them even better. People who are insistent on process make the systems hum, but if there aren't some resistant individuals on the team (including leadership), the organization will become ingrown. I'm sure my bias is showing, but I think those leaders need to do some soul-searching and create a culture where both ends bring their best, respecting each other and valuing the

Fresh ideas are essential to a vibrant, passionate organization.

contributions of people on the team who are very unlike them. A new and different perspective to solve a problem, propel a product, or serve customers isn't wrong just because it doesn't immediately conform to the existing rules and procedures. Fresh ideas are essential to a vibrant, passionate organization. They might not always generate growth and improvement, but stubbornly maintaining the status quo almost never does.

Compassion often compels employees to ignore the rules so they can provide exemplary service. Southwest Airlines is known for customer service. Many people have heard of the incident in 2011 when a man booked a flight to Denver to see his grandson for the last time. Heavy traffic delayed the man's trip to the airport. The flight was scheduled to leave, but the Southwest pilot somehow knew how important the trip was to the man, so he delayed takeoff until the man could arrive and board the plane.

Zappos, the online shoe store, has a similar story. Because of a family member's death, a customer was late returning a pair of shoes. The customer service team not only provided a courier to pick up the shoes, they also sent the customer a bouquet of flowers and a note expressing their condolences.

Every organization follows certain processes that have been established and refined over time. Change in those areas is rare, and it requires a spectacularly brilliant new idea! Yet we should always be on the lookout for ways to do things better so the team is more energized and the customers served more effectively. No organization thrives when everyone is resistant to process; they need some people who value stability and repetition. And no organization thrives when everyone is insistent; they will never excel without an infusion of creativity and enthusiasm.

CALLING OR CONSENSUS

Let me tell a story about a remarkable leader: One of the main tasks of a leader is to communicate in a way that inspires the commitment of the people on the team. In the vast majority of cases, building consensus is essential if the purpose is to be fulfilled. Leaders simply aren't likely to succeed if their key people don't buy in. Yet occasionally situations arise where the best leaders know they have to buck this trend, resist the voice of consensus, and perhaps march alone.

Truett Cathy is the late founder of Chick-fil-A. He built one of the most successful fast-food chains in America, and he was admired not only for his business acuity but also for his generosity. Years ago, he was asked to speak at Berry College in Rome, Georgia. During the visit, Truett and his wife Jeannette were shown a beautiful parcel of college property in the lush green hills of North Georgia. The property had a magnificent chapel, stone dormitories, a library, a chapel, a gym, and a building housing several classrooms . . . all sitting empty. It had originally been a boarding school for children, the result of Martha Berry's vision in 1902 to provide a school for those who had no other access to education. Over time, however, the maintenance costs had climbed to $2 million a year—far beyond what the school could afford. Berry College was going to put the property up for sale, and they wanted to show it to the Cathys first.

As soon as she saw it, Jeannette was moved. Later she said, "I felt like I was on holy ground." She and Truett believed God was calling them to buy the abandoned land, restore the buildings, and transform them into a place that would have a dramatic impact on individuals and families.

The next day, Truett was back in Atlanta, excited to follow his normal process of involving his executive committee in the decision. When he told them about his vision for the property, however, their response was hesitant, even resistant. He tried to persuade them by taking them on a road trip see the property. After walking over the land and seeing the buildings, they were even less convinced that Truett should purchase it. They weren't defiant, selfish people. Their hearts were in the right place, but they simply couldn't get on the same page with Truett's vision for the property. Truett thanked them for their honest feedback, but he decided to purchase the property anyway. He knew his calling was more important than the consensus of his committee. He and Jeannette bought the property and created WinShape Foundation to "create experiences that transform." From summer camps to marriage retreats, the staff at WinShape continues to teach biblical, practical principles of life.[31]

If Truett had followed the advice of his executive committee, WinShape wouldn't exist today, at least not in its present form. He understood that a leader's central calling isn't up for a vote. Consensus is always desirable, but not always possible. A leader should communicate his or her vision in a way that inspires enthusiasm and evokes action, but sometimes leaders have to go against the grain. In the attempt to get consensus, some leaders water down the vision and compromise the process until enough people finally say, "Okay, I guess we'll do it." That's not leadership, and that's not the kind of passion that moves organizations forward.

Consensus-driven decision-making might increase the popularity of leaders for a moment, but it decreases their potential. Eventually, however, a bold leader earns the respect of the team. I can imagine the response of the Chick-fil-A executive committee when Truett announced he was going ahead with the purchase of the Berry College property against their advice, but their respect for him only grew as they saw how the center changed people's lives.

If leaders sacrifice their vision on the altar of consensus, the world will miss something wonderful.

You may think this point is the antithesis of everything I've written about process. In some ways, it certainly seems that way, but my point is that the process, even the very important element of building consensus, isn't sacrosanct. On rare occasions, a leader simply must follow his instincts, even when no one else is excited or even understands his thinking. If leaders sacrifice their vision on the altar of consensus, the world will miss something wonderful. Don't do it. Know your purpose, let it propel you, communicate powerfully and winsomely, and don't let anything stop you.

This single-minded dedication to purpose and calling, of course, isn't an excuse for bullheaded leaders to disregard the input of their most trusted advisors. Going against their advice requires leaders to be more reflective about the benefits and costs, willing to bring people along later, and ready to admit when they realize they were wrong. It happens . . . believe me.

A PERSPECTIVE ON FAILURE

Effective processes don't eliminate failure, but they usually reduce it. And good leaders who implement processes aren't rattled by failure. Instead, they capitalize on it for the good of the organization. They realize every process can be improved, so they aren't defensive (or surprised) when plans fail. I believe failure is one of our most effective teachers. In our programs, we orchestrate "micro-failures" to help students learn how to respond in positive, productive ways. We find that most people are ashamed or defensive when they fail. When young professionals realize failure can teach them valuable lessons, their perspective changes and they aren't as afraid to take risks.

Failure, though, isn't the only good teacher. I've also studied the power of success. We often talk about the importance of momentum in sports, but it's just as important in work or school. Leaders can become "success enhancers." For instance, when a student comes home with a report card of three As, a B, and an F, parents almost universally focus first (and often only) on the F. It would be powerful to first encourage the student, "Tell me how you did so well in those three classes." The answer may tell the parent what is needed to turn the failing class around. But if the parents focus only on the bad grade, the success is overshadowed by criticism and perhaps shame. I'm not saying the parents should avoid addressing the failure. I'm only suggesting they will get a better response—more encouragement, more optimism, and more dedication to improvement—if they focus first on the success and draw lessons there that can be applied in the difficult class.

The same pattern applies in our relationships with the people on our teams. If someone succeeds in eight tasks and botches one, many of us are quick to criticize the failure without commenting on the victories. Instead, we can first discuss with the employee what led to all the success, and then connect those principles to the failure. This leadership concept is very simple, but it can be revolutionary.

BLEND AND BALANCE

At Ritz-Carlton, the management has a finely tuned process to assure outstanding customer service. Every employee is trained to notice the needs of guests and do everything they can do to meet those needs. Customer service isn't just the responsibility of the front desk and the concierge—it's everybody's job. Their internal mantra is: "We are ladies and gentlemen serving ladies and gentlemen." One of their most remarkable corporate policies is that every employee is authorized to spend up to $2000 to satisfy the desires or meet the needs of any guest at any time. This policy is in effect for every employee, from the CEO to those in housekeeping, on their 73 properties in 24 countries.

In an interview with *Forbes* a few years ago, the company's president and CEO, Simon Cooper, explained Ritz-Carlton's vision of customer service:

> "The concept is to do something, to create an absolutely wonderful stay for a guest. Significantly, there is no assumption that it's because there is a problem. It could be that someone finds out it's a guest's birthday, and the next thing you know

there's champagne and cake in the room. A lot of the stuff that crosses my desk is not that they overcame a problem but that they used their $2,000 to create an outstanding experience. There are stories about hiring a carpenter to build a shoe tree for a guest; a laundry manager who couldn't get the stain out of a dress after trying twice flying up from Puerto Rico to New York to return the dress personally; or when in Dubai a waiter overheard a gentleman musing with his wife, who was in a wheelchair, that it was a shame he couldn't get her down to the beach. The waiter told maintenance, who passed word, and the next afternoon there was a wooden walkway down the beach to a tent that was set up for them to have dinner in. That's not out of the ordinary, and the general manager didn't know about it until it was built."[32]

Ritz-Carlton has created a culture with a powerful blend of clear, repeatable processes and not merely the freedom, but the *expectation* that every employee should be incredibly creative in finding ways to make their guests thrilled to have booked a stay at their hotels. They have gone far beyond rules and systems to empower employees from the executive suite to those who clean rooms or bus tables to think outside the box and use company resources to make guests happy. Can your company and mine take steps in this direction? Of course we can.

The steps to create a powerful blend of process and creativity include everything we've said in this chapter:

• First, recognize your skewed perception (your innate bias) as it relates to process. Without this insight, you'll stay stuck in your limitations.

- Learn to value the contributions of people who are on the other end of the spectrum from you. They have a lot to offer . . . if you'll invite them to speak up and you're willing to listen.

- Take steps to compensate for your bias. If you're insistent on process, be sure to ask creative people for their input on thinking outside the box; if you're resistant to process, applaud the contributions of those who are creating replicable methods; and if you're adaptable, help your team members at both extremes appreciate those who are so different from them (and who often annoy them so much).

- Remind yourself often to value the other perspective. I need to put a note on my wall that tells me, "Value the process," and insistent leaders need one that says, "Invite new ideas."

When we don't acknowledge the fact that we need glasses, we assume the way we see things is good and right and normal. The fact that you need glasses to see more clearly is not a flaw, but it is a flaw to remain blind when a clearer perspective is available. Being honest about our biases forces us to be vulnerable with our teams, but we're usually the last to admit our deficits. Great teams have a unity of purpose but not uniformity of perspective. We need each other, and we are most effective when we lean on each other.

Quality is never an accident; it is always the result of high intention,
sincere effort, intelligent direction and skillful execution;
it represents the wise choice of many alternatives.
—*William A. Foster*

TAKE A LOOK . . .

1.   From the descriptions in this chapter, would you say you are resistant, adaptable, or insistent in your approach to process? Explain your answer.

2.   How would the people on your team or in your organization identify your bias?

3.   Who are the people on your team who see process the same way you do? Who sees it from a different perspective? How do those differences affect your relationships and your team's performance?

4.   How might you implement a focus on success as the key to helping people respond to failure with more hope?

5.   What can you learn from the example of Ritz-Carlton?

6.   What are some specific things you can do to implement the steps to create a powerful blend of a process and creativity listed at the end of the chapter?

CHAPTER 5
PROFIT

An organization's culture of purpose answers the critical questions of who it is and why it exists. They have a culture of purpose beyond making a profit.
—*Punit Renjen, CEO of Deloitte Global*

Profit is how we tend to measure success and keep score, so it is a tough topic to address because it often clouds our viewpoint. In business, it almost always refers to the number that results when you deduct expenses from revenues. That's the point: it's a number. Other types of organizations may not use the term *profit*, but they are no less focused on target numbers. In nonprofits, the measure of success is often the *number* of people served through programs. In politics, it's first the vote count in order to win the election, and once elected, it's the votes needed to pass bills. Still numbers.

If a number—whether profit, people helped, or votes—isn't the ultimate measure of success, what is? As we saw in the opening chapter, our purpose needs to be bigger than ourselves. Our reason for getting up each day should be to have a positive impact on others. In business, money is a means to this end, but it's not the end.

Our measure of success necessarily influences our motivation. The singular pursuit of money is driven by pride, power, and the desire for acclaim—it's a way people keep score, a way they know they're winning. As we've said, titles, power, and approval aren't evil if they are byproducts of the desire to improve the lives of others, but when those become our primary motives, we begin to use people to get to our goals.

During the first years of our company, I had trouble thinking about our profits because I associated profits with greed. I didn't want to be "that guy obsessed with money" others talked about, so I felt uncomfortable with any conversation about making money. (Yeah, I know. It's hard to imagine a business owner who doesn't want to talk about profits!) I realized, though, that we couldn't grow and have an impact on more people unless we generated a profit. Our motive for making money was good and right: it was to fulfill our corporate purpose.

I don't think our company is unique. I believe every business should use profit as a means of improving the lives of others. In politics, the goal shouldn't be only to win the next election, but to win in order to create a culture of justice, opportunity, safety, and compassion. It's not as easy to effect change if you're not elected to do so. In nonprofits, effective fundraising isn't the end goal, but it's necessary for providing resources to help people in need.

A bigger purpose (the why) and a compelling value proposition (the how) determine the way we pursue our goals. The question we need to ask is this: *What am I willing to do to acquire the profits I need in order to achieve my others-centered purpose?* Are we willing to cut corners on quality to maximize profits, or do we charge a reasonable fee for our products or services, pay our employees and vendors fairly and on time, and develop a reputation for being honest and fair? We must consider these and probably a dozen other similar questions.

Jesus asked his closest followers, "For what does it profit a man to gain the whole world and forfeit his soul?"[33] His point is demonstrated by literary characters like Jay Gatsby (of *The Great Gatsby*) and Jordan Belfort (of *The Wolf of Wall Street*), who get it completely wrong. The relentless pursuit of money doesn't pay off with happiness and contentment. Instead, people who value wealth above all things poison their relationships and lose what's most valuable to them. They forfeit their souls as they become ingrown and self-absorbed, driven to have more or deeply discouraged when having more doesn't bring additional meaning to their lives. To be sure, on the way up when they appear to have it made, they're excited about the fame and power wealth promises. But history is littered with people whose lives eventually cratered because they loved money too much. They learned too late that money wasn't the problem; the problem was putting money above the purpose of having a positive impact on others.

Many people perceive profit as the ultimate finish line or the final score, but leaders need to see profit as only a measuring stick on the way to success.

CONNECTING PURPOSE AND PROFITS

I'm quite sure many in the business world disagree with my conclusion that money is never the ultimate measure of profit. They work for companies that talk all the time about shareholder dividends, stock prices, and executive compensation. In those companies, it seems money is everything. Those leaders would consider me "soft" on the realities of the business world, but that's a shortsighted perspective.

The way people feel about their company or products makes a difference on the bottom line. Most millennials want to work in companies that enhance their personal development. To them, a job is not only about the salary. They gravitate toward companies that have stated values that are like their own, and they prefer to buy from companies that go to great lengths to connect with them. In an article by Rakuten Marketing, Daniel James states that millennials expect a marketing experience, and then explains:

"YOLO (You Only Live Once). FOMO (Fear of Missing Out). These are phrases that Millennials love to live by, whether it be staying out just a little later with friends on a weekend night to see what the evening may bring, or take a last-minute vacation somewhere. The message is clear: Millennials value experiences over owning things. Not surprisingly, they prefer to have their marketing feel that way too. And make no mistake—experiential marketing *works*. According to a survey conducted by Factory360, a shocking 98% of participants felt more inclined to purchase a product when they participated in an experiential campaign."[34]

For any organization to thrive over an extended time, leaders must connect with the next generation. Connecting with millennials and Generation Z, whether as customers or employees (and most likely both), is important. Today's generation chooses companies to do business with the way previous generations chose charities. When people spend their time or money with a business, they want it to say something about who they are and what they believe. Young people want their workplace to provide meaning, not just money.

Young people want their workplace to provide meaning, not just money.

The popularity of TOMS shoes is a case in point. The company's shoes are, by most accounts, plain and not very attractive. However, the company has captured the hearts of young people (and plenty who aren't so young) by their commitment to provide a pair to a shoeless person for every pair purchased. Customers realize that buying a pair of

TOMS shoes isn't only about covering their feet; it's also about putting shoes on someone with bare feet. The bigger purpose drives the reason to make, market, and sell shoes, and it attracts consumers who have a heart for hurting people and see this as an effective (and easy) way to make a difference in someone's life.

Let's face it: most companies don't have a product that instantly connects customers to a higher purpose. They have to think of other ways to communicate their corporate values. A few years ago, Nordstrom announced in the fall that they would not be open on Thanksgiving Day. Other retailers had started opening earlier and earlier to get a jump on Black Friday sales, but Nordstrom had a different priority. While other stores spent millions to advertise they would be open on the holiday, Nordstrom spent their advertising dollars saying they would close Thanksgiving Day because they valued their employees' time with their families. Their stores would be open for business and available to customers the following day. For Nordstrom, communicating their values was more important than getting a jump on sales. Companies that communicate (and live by) a higher purpose and strong values are the ones that ultimately win.

Here are some mission or vision statements of a few outstanding companies:

- Delta Air Lines: "We—Delta's employees, customers, and community partners—together form a force for positive local and global change, dedicated to bettering standards of living and the environment where we and our customers live and work."

- Amazon (since 1995): "To be Earth's most customer-centric company, where customers can find and discover anything they might want to buy online, and endeavors to offer its customers the lowest possible prices."

- Facebook: "Bring the world closer together."

- Coca-Cola: "To refresh the world…To inspire moments of optimism and happiness…To create value and make a difference."

- Google: "To organize the world's information and make it universally accessible and useful."

- JP Morgan Chase & Co.: "To be the best financial services company in the world. Because of our great heritage and excellent platform, we believe this is within our reach."

- General Electric: "Passionate, Curious, Resourceful, Accountable, Teamwork, Committed, Open, Energizing, Always with Unyielding Integrity."

These companies aren't saying they don't care about profits, and they certainly aren't so idealistic they would suggest that profits are dirty, wrong, or evil. Instead, they keep their eyes on a larger goal, and they use profits to achieve that goal. Their mission-minded owners see the connection between purpose and profits, and so do investors who may choose these publicly traded companies as much for their impact as their return on investment.

VIRTUE AND CAPITALISM

About the time our nation was founded, economist Adam Smith defined capitalism as a machine that takes private self-interest and organizes it to produce general prosperity. In more than two centuries since then, capitalism has proven to be magnificently successful. Almost without exception, the nations whose economies have been based on this economic model have seen advances in incomes, living conditions, health, and technology. Those based on something else, such as communism, have made far less progress, leading to oppression, unrest, and wide splits between the rich and poor.

One of the marvels of the modern world is the transformation of China's economy, beginning in 1978, from centrally-planned to more market-based, lifting more than 800 million people out of poverty.[35] Around the world the percentage of people living on $1 a day has declined by eighty percent in the same period, and the reason is the global rise of capitalism, especially in disadvantaged countries.

Arthur Brooks, the president of the conservative American Enterprise Institute, is a defender of capitalism, but he defends it on moral, not materialistic grounds. The moral health of an economic system can be measured by its capacity to help people instill meaning into their lives—to fulfill a higher purpose than making money.[36]

New York Times columnist David Brooks observes that the philosophers who shaped Western culture assumed people were fundamentally selfish, and that economic theory is based on the self-interested pursuit of wealth and power. Brooks, however, disagrees: "This worldview is clearly wrong. In real life, the push of selfishness is matched by the pull of empathy and altruism. This is not Hallmark card sentimentalism but scientific fact: As babies our neural connections are built by love and care. We have evolved to be really good at cooperation and empathy. We are strongly motivated to teach and help others."

Brooks asserts that there are "two lenses" people use to view poverty and prosperity: the economic lens or the moral lens. When people are motivated primarily for financial gain, they fail to follow "their natural bias toward reciprocity, service and cooperation." He draws a stark contrast between others-focused and self-focused cost-benefit calculus. He concludes:

> "To be a good citizen, to be a good worker, you often have to make an altruistic commitment to some group or ideal, which

will see you through those times when your job of citizenship is hard and frustrating. Whether you are a teacher serving students or a soldier serving your country or a clerk who likes your office mates, the moral motivation is much more powerful than the financial motivations. Arrangements that arouse the financial lens alone are just messing everything up."[37]

President George W. Bush often talked about the importance of "compassionate conservatism." I think at least one component of it is what I'd call "generous capitalism."

If having a higher purpose than financial gain is important, is it possible to work for a company, or for a boss, that obviously cares only about money? Yes, absolutely, but you have to realize you'll be swimming upstream most of the time. When all the messages we hear from those above us and around us are self-interested ones, it requires us to be clear and strong in our passion for a higher purpose. We need to find some friends who will keep supporting us and injecting us with courage and hope. Sometimes the people around us notice that we've put on a different set of glasses to look at the company, profits, our team, and customers. When we tell them about our purpose, they might think we've lost our minds ... but then again, they might feel inspired to try some new lenses, too.

If money serves meaning, money becomes very important in reaching the company's potential.

When leaders have a powerful purpose, they don't have to shy away from financial goals. If money serves meaning, money becomes very important in reaching the company's potential. When I was in college,

I was part of an amazing organization, UGA HEROs, which provides resources for children in Georgia who have been affected by HIV/AIDS. Like every other charitable organization on campus, we were excited about the impact we could have. But we also realized our impact would be limited by the amount of money we raised. In the past, we had seen fundraising as secondary to our mission of caring for kids, but we began to discover that it was essential to our mission. We set clear, high, measurable goals for fundraising—higher than we'd ever had before. We now had a passion to raise money *so that* we could help more children. We quadrupled the amount of money we raised, which enabled us to provide exponentially more resources and services to the children. By having a better perspective on money as the means to the end, we accomplished far more than before.

On a very practical level, I recently realized I needed to let the people in our company, ADDO Worldwide, know more about our finances. In one of our staff meetings, I showed a slide that detailed our monthly revenues and expenses for the past three years, as well as our projections for the coming year. After the meeting, three people pulled me aside to tell me how helpful it was for them to understand the big picture of our finances. Each of them let me know in their own way that they could now connect the revenues and expenses on their projects to the overall economics of the company, and that insight unlocked and unleashed their enthusiasm to do an even better job. For a long time, I had been hesitant to communicate our need for profit, but I finally learned to connect profit to our purpose. I couldn't connect the dots for my team, however, until I connected them for myself.

IN GOOD COMPANY

Whether you're a leader in a consulting firm, a restaurant, a clothing store, an oil company, a heating and air conditioning company, or any other firm, your employees know money is important to the organization. But you need to make sure they know it's not ultimately important. Your job is to explain how profits are essential to enable the company to have a greater impact for good in the lives of customers and clients.

This role of leadership isn't something I dreamed up. It's a truth all good leaders come to realize. Some of the finest executives in the business world came to this conclusion first. For example:

- "At the end of the day, you want to be profitable, but that's not the meaning of life" (Daniel Lamarre, Cirque du Soleil).

- "To be truly successful, companies need to have a corporate mission that is bigger than making a profit" (Marc Benioff, Salesforce).

- "We have to bring this world back to sanity and put the greater good ahead of self-interest" (Paul Polman, Unilever).

- "Essentially being a for-profit creates opportunity for doing greater good. And financial success as a for-profit with a social conscious carries greater credibility with your peers, potentially influencing actions of other businesses" (Brian Walker, Herman Miller).

- "When you're surrounded by people who share a passionate commitment around a common purpose, anything is possible" (Howard Schultz, Starbucks).

- "Just as people cannot live without eating, so a business cannot live without profits. But most people don't live to eat, and neither must businesses live just to make profits" (John Mackey, Whole Foods).

- "Money motivates neither the best people, nor the best in people. It can move the body and influence the mind, but it cannot touch the heart or move the spirit; that is reserved for belief, principle, and morality" (Dee Hock, Visa).

- "People want to do well and do good. They want to understand how they're making a difference in the world. Things change all the time, but your organization's purpose transcends any individual product or service" (Mark Weinberger, EY).

- "The real goal of what we're doing is to have a positive impact on the world" (Ed Catmull, Pixar).[38]

These executives aren't lightweights, and they aren't soft on the importance of profits. But they're convinced profits serve a deeper meaning.

LOOKING PAST MONEY

Profit is certainly a way to keep score, but we put a damper on our people's passion if they think it's the only score that matters. We need to talk about the higher purpose we've written in our mission or vision statement, and we need to continually remind our people that profits enable us to provide more products, offer more services, give customers a better experience, and make life better for everyone involved.

Perhaps the highest goal for leaders is to uncover our people's inherent desire to make a difference in the lives of others, inspire them to care about more than a paycheck, and show them how profits are a means to those higher ends. This connection is important in every endeavor: business, nonprofits, politics, and churches. When profits serve purpose, we have nothing to apologize for when we try to make more money (assuming, of course, that we are honest and fair in all our dealings).

Many years ago, I heard a speech that I've never forgotten. The speaker took two quarters out of his pocket and put them right in front of his eyes. He explained that many see only money, blinding us to everything else wonderful and beautiful in the world. He then extended his arms, holding the quarters far from his eyes. He said that when we see money in the context of everything else in our lives, it's still important, but not supremely important. It no longer blinds us to the things that really matter: the relationships, opportunities, and joys around us. Money isn't the problem, although our perspective of money may be a huge problem. I've never forgotten that image. I hope you won't either.

It's not "How can we make more?" It's "How can we do more?"
— Neil Blumenthal, Warby Parker

TAKE A LOOK . . .

1. How do the leaders in your company measure success? What are some ways they show what they care most about?

2.   Do you believe most people are looking for more than a paycheck when they go to work? Are they really looking for a place where they can invest their lives for a higher purpose? Explain your answer.

3.   What should be the connection between capitalism and an organization's values?

4.   What are some practical ways you can help the people on your team connect the dots between profit and purpose? What difference do you think it will make for them to understand this connection?

6. Do you agree or disagree with the statement: "Money is never the ultimate measure of profit"? Explain your answer.

7. Think about the illustration at the end of the chapter. Where are the quarters in relation to your eyes? What, if anything, needs to change?

CHAPTER 6
POWER

*Servant leadership is all about making the goals clear and then rolling your
sleeves up and doing whatever it takes to help people win.
In that situation, they don't work for you; you work for them.*
—Ken Blanchard

News flash: Like profit, there's nothing inherently right or wrong
about power. The questions we should ask are, "Why do we pursue power?" and "What do we do with power when we have it?"

In the right hands, power can accomplish enormous good. In fact,
little good can be accomplished without someone wielding power.
But the history of nations, corporations, organizations, and families
shows that when power is used inappropriately, damage can be deep
and lasting. In reaction to this misuse or abuse, some people insist on
creating an environment in which no one has any power. The concept
may sound good and noble, but it is naïve and just doesn't work. Someone always has power, whether it's formally acquired or delegated, or
it's informal and assumed by another means.

Many of us have been on teams where the person others looked to
for wisdom and direction wasn't the team leader; it was someone without the title, yet who had earned the respect of the group. When he or
she talked, the rest of the team listened. Even with no formal authority,
the person had plenty of influence.

Or maybe you've been on a team where the person with the most
clout wasn't respected at all. Perhaps it was someone who intimidated

the leader and the rest of the team with biting wit, cynicism, and icy stares. Power can come in many different forms. Quite often, the person with the most influence in a room isn't the one who called the meeting, whose name is on the corner office door, or who is sitting at the head of the table.

The sweet spot of power is hard to find. Some people are afraid of power because they've been hurt by others who abused positions of power. Others have the opposite reaction: they crave power, but their motive is completely self-focused—it's about their career advancement, their raises, their reputations. These people do whatever it takes to gain it, and they exhaust all resources to retain it. Integrity and the good of the team take a backseat to their insatiable thirst for power. (At this point, you may be picturing a specific person's face!) When our perspective on power is correct, our means of acquiring it and using it will be honorable, gracious, and productive.

> **Many people perceive power as inherently abusive, but leaders need to see how it can be used to elevate and empower others.**

LOSING AND REGAINING POWER

As the leader of our company, I try to use my power in a number of ways. In my position, I want to present a clear perspective about our purpose and each priority as we face new opportunities. I need to give our team a sense of consistency and cohesion so they understand how today's priority fits with the past and the future.

It hasn't always been this way. For a while, three of us shared leadership of the company. We assumed (or at least, I assumed) good intentions would enable us to overcome any difficulties. I was wrong. During that time, we sometimes had relatively minor differences in our sense of purpose and our priority, but even then, the mist from the conflicting messages among the three of us produced a dense fog on our team. And too often, we didn't have only minor differences—we saw problems and new opportunities very differently. The lack of a coherent voice of leadership created tremendous tension, and it drove our team crazy.

The differing messages caused people to wonder if their marching orders were going to be changed in the next meeting, the next phone call, or the next text. They felt frustrated, and they were often paralyzed by indecision. We were like a dysfunctional family when a child gets an answer from one parent she doesn't want to hear and goes to the other parent to get a different response. Even when one of us gave crystal clear direction, team members were afraid to act because they anticipated a conflicting message from one of the other two. Each of the three of us would wonder why our people didn't do what we told them to do, so we were frustrated with them.

Without saying so overtly, the three leaders were each asking team members for loyalty, so they felt torn. Instead of devoting their time and energies to activities that advanced the company's purpose, they spent far too much time trying to figure out how to respond to each of the leaders, talking to one another about the conflicting messages, and trying to manage the chaos. They felt like pawns in a three-person chess game. All of this would have been difficult enough with only two leaders. With three, it was a disaster. The problem, of course, wasn't that we had multiple leaders; the problem was that the three of us weren't aligned in our purpose, the way we treated people, and our use of power to advance our organization's goals.

When I was describing this era of our company's life to a friend, he asked, "Didn't you see what was happening?" Yes, I saw it, but two things happened: I didn't want to wade into the conflict because I was sure it would explode if I confronted the problem directly, and I had too much confidence in my people skills and my ability to assuage the hurt feelings of the people on our team. I had a lot of relational capital with people who reported to me. I thought that was enough, so I let the simmering chaos continue and tried to mitigate the damage. Finally, I came to a sobering conclusion: I had become part of the problem, not part of a solution.

It all came to a head when the conflict of perspectives and purposes became unavoidable and we decided to make a major change in leadership. At that point, the fog in my own mind cleared, and I saw with clarity how I had perpetuated the craziness. Failure can be one of the best teachers, and I learned a lot from this difficult season of our company's history. I had thought my relational skills had made things at least tolerable, if not good, for the people on our team. When I saw things more clearly, I realized my voice had been only one of three, and I had contributed significantly to everyone's frustrations.

Near the time of the transition, we asked our staff for feedback on how the team was functioning. One comment was indicative of the others: "We don't have clarity. Leadership needs to flex their authoritative muscles more—being clear, honest, and direct. I want to know who's in charge around here!"

We finally settled who had organizational control, and from that point I could speak with clarity about our values and direction. In many conversations with people over the years, I've found that some want authority over them because it gives them a sense of safety, but others say they don't want to be under authority at all. My conviction is that everyone on a team needs someone to be in charge, but they need leaders who bring out the best in them, stimulate their creativity, and value their unique contribution. We had tried to have a flat organizational structure with shared authority, and in doing so we had created a mess. Our people longed for a leader to step up, provide a definitive message of purpose, and give them tracks to run on. For teams to function well, a sense of authority is essential.

SERVANT LEADERSHIP

I believe a leader's productive use of power is directly proportional to his or her emotional health. When leaders feel insecure, they invariably are "too" something: too unclear or too demanding, too gentle or too harsh, too involved in everyone's personal life and job or too aloof and detached. Secure leaders don't use intimidation to control people, and they aren't afraid

> **When leaders feel insecure, they invariably are "too" something: too unclear or too demanding, too gentle or too harsh, too involved in everyone's personal life and job or too aloof and detached.**

to give direction and make hard calls. They realize their role is to help all team members feel valued, acquire skills and experience, and contribute to fulfill the team's purpose. Secure leaders act as servant leaders.

The leaders I most admire serve their teams. I've thought through and spoken about the concept of servant leadership so much that it's second nature to me, but I've learned it's foreign to many people. To me, good leadership *is* servant leadership—they're the same thing. The term was first coined by Robert Greenleaf in his 1970 essay, "The Servant as Leader." He explains:

"The servant-leader is a servant first.... It begins with the natural feeling that one wants to serve, to serve first. Then conscious choice brings one to aspire to lead. That person is sharply different from one who is leader first, perhaps because of the need to assuage an unusual power drive or to acquire material possessions. For such it will be a later choice to serve—after leadership is established. The leader-first and the servant-first are two extreme types. Between them there are shadings and blends that are part of the infinite variety of human nature."

To Greenleaf, the outcomes of the two forms of leadership are clear. His series of questions sharpens the contrasts:

"The difference manifests itself in the care taken by the servant-first leader to make sure that the other people's highest priority needs are being served. The best test, and difficult to administer, is: Do those served grow as persons? Do they, while being served, become healthier, wiser, freer, more autonomous, more likely themselves to become servants? And, what is the effect on the least privileged in society; will they benefit, or, at least, not be further deprived?"[39]

A power differential is inherent in any company or organization. It's a fact, so the question isn't how to get rid of the differential, but how to use our power for good. Traditional forms of leadership accrue power for status, wealth, control, or some other self-focused benefit. Servant leadership is others-centered; leaders are committed to invest their authority, wisdom, and talents to serve their people.

How does this look in practice? Servant-leaders have a simple but revolutionary commitment: "My life for yours" instead of "My life for me." Dozens of times each day they see they have a choice: to listen to someone or pass them by, to say thank you for a contribution or to ignore it, to ask a second or third follow-up question or to make a quick assessment and move on, to tailor a task to a person or to hand out random assignments, to wash the dishes when a spouse has had a long day or to collapse in front of the television, and on and on and on.

Servant leaders have grasped "the upside-down principle at the heart of the universe":

- The last shall be first and the first shall be last.

- To have true riches, give generously.

- To have real power, give it away.

- If we try to save our lives, we'll lose them, but if we lose our lives for others, we'll find them.

- To experience the relief of forgiveness, we admit we're deeply flawed.

- The proud will be humbled and the humble will be exalted.[40]

Yes, these are all biblical concepts, but they aren't limited to church, Bible study groups, or private devotions— we see them played out every day in our homes and offices. Real love, joy, and fulfillment come to us only when we sacrifice a moment of convenience to inject kindness, appreciation, love, joy, and meaning into someone else's life. Over and

Real love, joy, and fulfillment come to us only when we sacrifice a moment of convenience to inject kindness, appreciation, love, joy, and meaning into someone else's life.

over throughout the day we have the chance to make the decision: My life for yours.

When we think of the most glowing examples of servant leadership, most of us would identify Jesus, Gandhi, Martin Luther King, Jr., and Mother Teresa. We don't need to be Christians or Hindus to realize these remarkable people made a profound and lasting impact on the world. Each of them lived by the principle of servant leadership, even when they weren't applauded for it. In fact, several of them suffered severe opposition and privation. Three of them were martyred for their service to others, and the other died in poverty.

The point is that servant leaders leave a powerful and lasting impact, but they often pay a price. Serving others necessarily means we deny something to ourselves so we can give something to the people around us. We sacrifice time, money, convenience, energy, and perhaps even our reputations for the good of others. Is it worth it? I'd say so. The thrill of seeing another person flourish, and maybe even witnessing a life turned around, is worth more than a little more money, a little more time, a little more applause, and a little more comfort.

THE COURAGE OF A SERVANT LEADER

Servant leaders aren't passive or wimpy. They know that serving the underserved sometimes requires them to boldly confront those who are harming the vulnerable. Today, we still wrestle with elements of racism in the United States, but only a few decades ago, the struggle was far more fierce. Martin Luther King, Jr. led a nonviolent movement that often resulted in arrests and beatings, yet he continued to speak boldly and clearly for the cause of racial justice.

In April of 1963, King was arrested for protesting segregation in Birmingham, Alabama. He was accused of being an outsider stirring up trouble in the city. In response, he wrote one of the most powerful letters in American history. In part, it reads:

"I am in Birmingham because injustice is here. . . . We have waited for more than three hundred and forty years for our God-given and constitutional rights. . . . I guess it is easy for those who have never felt the stinging darts of segregation to say 'wait.' But when you have seen vicious mobs lynch your mothers and fathers at will and drown your sisters and brothers at whim; when you have seen hate-filled policemen curse, kick, brutalize, and even kill your black brothers and sisters with impunity; when you see the vast majority of your twenty million Negro brothers smothering in an airtight cage of poverty in the midst of an affluent society; when you suddenly find your tongue twisted and your speech stammering as you seek to explain to your six-year-old daughter why she cannot go to the public amusement park that has just been advertised on television, and see tears welling up in her little eyes when she is told that Funtown is closed to colored children, and see the depressing clouds of inferiority begin to form in her little mental sky, and see her begin to distort her little personality by unconsciously developing a bitterness toward white people; when you have to concoct an answer for a five-year-old son asking in agonizing pathos, 'Daddy, why do white people treat colored people so mean?'; . . . when you are harried by day and haunted by night by the fact that you are a Negro, living constantly at tiptoe stance, never quite knowing what to expect next, and plagued with inner fears and outer resentments; when you are forever fighting a degenerating sense of 'nobodyness'—then you will understand why we find it difficult to wait. There comes a time when the cup of endurance runs over and men are no longer willing to be plunged into an abyss of injustice where they experience the bleakness of corroding despair. I hope, sirs, you can understand our legitimate and unavoidable impatience."

To show that he wasn't fuming in rage and wasn't threatening the leaders or the people of Birmingham, Dr. King ended his letter:

"If I have said anything in this letter that is an overstatement of the truth and is indicative of an unreasonable impatience, I beg you to forgive me. If I have said anything in this letter that is an understatement of the truth and is indicative of my having a patience that makes me patient with anything less than brotherhood, I beg God to forgive me."[41]

Dr. King's house was bombed, he was threatened, beaten and arrested, and he endured the taunts of countless people on his marches, but he refused to stop speaking out and standing against injustice. If you care about people, if you are a servant leader, it doesn't matter whether you are black, white, brown, Republican, Democrat, Christian, Hindu, Jew, Muslim, or agnostic—you will sometimes need to say things people don't want to hear. You speak up, not because you don't love them, but because you do. Dr. King didn't have positional power in Birmingham and other cities throughout the South, but he had plenty of earned influence.

MOTIVE AND POWER

In itself, power is neither right nor wrong, good nor bad, moral nor immoral. The use of power takes on different qualities depending on our motives and methods of using it. No matter how we got into our positions of power, we can choose to use our platform to develop others so they lead successful, fulfilling lives.

Many people assume ambition is wrong . . . or at least suspect. It's the same principle: Ambition is also amoral, either good or bad depending on the motives. If leaders strive for more influence so they can serve more people and have a greater impact on them, then ambition has been harnessed for good purposes. I hope to climb the ladder of success so I can turn around to help others climb higher, too. It's very easy, though, to deceive ourselves about our motives. We are wise to invite insightful, trustworthy people to observe our lives, ask hard questions, and give us honest feedback.

The story of Nelson Mandela says a lot about servant leadership. He grew up in South Africa during the dark days of racial segregation known as apartheid. He became involved in an anti-apartheid movement, but the government didn't allow dissent. He was arrested, charged with inciting workers' strikes and leaving the country without permission, and convicted. The prosecution called for the death penalty, but he was sentenced to life in prison instead. He was sent to Robben Island in 1964 and spent the next eighteen years crafting his political philosophy and strategy . . . in case he was ever released. Mandela almost lost his sight in the glaring sun of hard labor. In 1982, he was transferred to another prison. At the time, the conflict between blacks and whites escalated in South Africa. Many predicted a bloody civil war.

By 1988, while still a prisoner, Mandela had become a leader of his movement. After P.W. Botha, the white nationalist party leader, suffered a stroke, he was replaced by F.W. de Klerk, who invited Mandela to a meeting to seek a solution to the violence. Shortly after this meeting, de Klerk granted Mandela an unconditional release.

The two leaders from very different backgrounds began serious negotiations, and after several years of talks they forged a solution:

the release of political prisoners, granting blacks the right to vote, and restrictions on weapons. Mandela's positions were attacked by most of the whites and the black extremists. Still, he held his ground. In 1994, Mandela ran on the national ballot, and with the support of millions of blacks, he became President of South Africa. With skill and wisdom, he led the transition from apartheid rule by the white minority to multicultural democracy. The civil war, which appeared certain, never happened. Violence, police repression, and recriminations were addressed by the Truth and Reconciliation Commission. People were invited to speak the brutal truth about what they'd suffered, and many of them chose to forgive, to heal, and to turn the page toward a better future.

Mandela could have become hardened and bitter in the stark prison on Robben Island, but instead, he carved a new direction for his homeland. With amazing humility, he observed, "It is better to lead from behind and to put others in front, especially when you celebrate victory when nice things occur. You take the front line when there is danger. Then people will appreciate your leadership." He also said, "Real leaders must be ready to sacrifice all for the freedom of their people."

Mandela was willing to sacrifice years in prison, and when he got out, he didn't give in to a natural thirst for vengeance. Instead, he put the good of others first: he worked with his enemies to create a better future for his people—people of all colors. During those years in prison, he longed for power, not to oppress his oppressors, but to create a nation of justice, forgiveness, prosperity, and hope.

Servant leadership isn't foreign to the corporate world. A recent *Inc.* magazine article described the leadership philosophy of Melissa Reiff, CEO of The Container Store. She was still new to the position, but her fingerprints were already on the corporate environment. Reiff explained, "We continuously strive to create a better, more innovative and compelling place to shop and to work, for the near and long-term success of our company. That includes a relentless focus on doing what's right for ALL of our stakeholders by operating our business through the lens of our Foundation Principles and a commitment to conscious leadership."

Reiff infuses her interactions with her philosophy of servant leadership. One of her principles is: "Communication IS Leadership." She strives for "daily execution of practicing consistent, reliable, predictable, effective, thoughtful, compassionate, and yes, even courteous communication." At the Container Store, Reiff and her team want every employee throughout the company to know "absolutely everything." As they state on their website: "Nothing makes someone feel more a part of a team than knowing everything has been communicated to them. We know that some information we share could fall into competitors' hands, but the advantages far outweigh the risks."[42]

This perspective on leadership isn't rare. The same *Inc.* article cited *Fortune*'s annual "100 Best Companies to Work For" and noted that the top brands "have grasped the immense power that is generated from putting people [employees] ahead of profits through shared values like authenticity, intrapreneurship, freedom and ownership, community, and collaboration. And servant leaders, naturally, have leveraged this emotional currency as the only sustainable model for the future of work."[43]

Some of the sharpest minds in the business world insist the principles and practices of servant leadership aren't ancillary to building a great company; they're essential. Here are a few comments:

- "The companies that survive are the ones that work out what they uniquely can give to the world—not just growth or money but their excellence, their respect for others, or their ability to make people happy" (Charles Handy, *The Search for Meaning*).

- "Leadership is not an affair of the head. Leadership is an affair of the heart.... Of all the things that sustain a leader over time, love is the most lasting. The best-kept secret of successful leaders is love: staying in love with leading, with the people who do the work, with what their organizations produce, and with those who honor the organization by using its work" (James Kouzes and Barry Posner, *The Leadership Challenge*).

- "You can have anything you want in life if you just help enough other people get what they want" (Zig Ziglar).

- "My research debunks the myth that many people seem to have ... that you become a leader by fighting your way to the top. Rather, you become a leader by helping others to the top. Helping your employees is as important as, and many times more so than, trying to get the most work out of them" (William Cohen, *The Stuff of Heroes: The Eight Universal Laws of Leadership*).

- "Your rewards in life will be in direct proportion to the value of your service to others" (Brian Tracy, *The 100 Absolutely Unbreakable Laws of Business Success*).

- "If leadership serves only the leader, it will fail. Ego satisfaction, financial gain, and status can all be valuable tools for a leader, but if they become the only motivations, they will eventually destroy a leader. Only when service for a common good is the primary purpose are you truly leading" (Sheila Murray Bethel, *Making a Difference: 12 Qualities That Make You a Leader*).[44]

CEOs and other top corporate leaders are in a position to shape the culture of their organizations; the corporate culture in the departments down the organizational chart probably won't be better than the top leader's. Therefore, leaders need to avoid making assumptions that their way is the only way . . . and always the right way. They need to ask for input, perhaps anonymous input, from all levels of employees to find out what kind of culture they're creating. Then, with courage and grace, they can make changes from the top management team down. Otherwise, it becomes too convenient to measure sales, products, and margins without considering the health of the culture being created, and the organization will ultimately suffer for it.

Mid-level managers often have the most difficult job of being servant leaders. They feel squeezed between quotas and expectations from the top while trying to create a healthy, motivated, valued team around them. They rarely can make a significant difference in the culture above them, yet they need to have integrity as they respond to upper management while still being committed to protect the people on their teams. Being a servant leader in a driven, demanding corporation always produces a lot of tension. Recognizing this reality is the first step in finding the wisdom to live in it each day.

Frontline employees don't have positions of authority and power, but they too can exercise enormous influence by their attitudes, kindness, and attention to detail. Most leaders can provide numerous examples of how one person on a team can either heal or poison all the others. All of us have choices, dozens of times each day, to be servants or to be selfish. In every interaction and every decision, we can choose to live by "My life for yours" or "My life for me."

Viktor Frankl endured years in a Nazi concentration camp. He watched people around him lose hope and die, and he saw others drop dead of exhaustion. In his account of these horrific years, he wrote,

"Everything can be taken from a man but one thing: the last of the human freedoms—to choose one's attitude in any given set of circumstances, to choose one's own way."[45]

All of us live with pressure, but very few suffer the stress Frankl endured. If Viktor Frankl can look at his life through that lens and make good and noble choices in a concentration camp, we can make them where we live and work.

> *The real power lies in service to others.*
> —*Cheryl Bachelder*

TAKE A LOOK . . .

1. How have you seen power used in an organization to build, strengthen, stimulate, and empower people?

2. How have you seen power intimidate and tear people down?

3. How would you define and describe servant leadership?

4. Who is a leader you know who exemplifies servant leadership? How does that person live by "My life for yours"? Describe the impact this person has on others.

5. What is your position in your organization? How do you live with the tension between the pressure to produce and the principles of servant leadership?

6. If you implement these principles and practices (or commit to doing them better), what will be the benefits? What are some costs?

7. What changes, if any, do you need to make to be a better servant leader?

CHAPTER 7

POSITIONING

Positioning is an art. Great positioning tells a compelling,
attention grabbing story—a story that resonates with your audience.
— *Rebel Brown*

When I was a senior in high school, I worked with a group of representatives from our class to build a float for the homecoming parade. We spent hours building our float at my friend Will's house. We framed the float with chicken wire on a flatbed trailer and filled the structure with colorful tissue paper. The float looked great, but there was a problem: whenever we moved the trailer, some pieces of tissue paper would loosen and fall out. The guys in the group weren't bothered by this. We just thought it was part of the texture and aesthetic of the float. However, the girls hated it. In fact, they insisted we cover the float with Saran Wrap® to hold the pieces of tissue in place. We all went along with their plan, and one problem was solved: no more loose tissue paper. But to me, there was now a bigger problem—the float looked hideous!

At the time, I didn't have the strength to stand up, use my diplomacy skills, and lead the group to a different decision. So instead of suggesting a reasonable fix for our ugly float, I hatched an alternate plan. I got some of the guys together and suggested we sabotage our own float on the morning of the parade. We'd spray-paint it to say things like, "Seniors Suck!" This plan would accomplish two goals: First, it would make it seem like the junior class was behind the destruction of our float, absolving us of any responsibility, and second, it would force our group to remove the Saran Wrap® without enough time to replace it before the parade. The float would look as bad as my fellow schemers intended, and the juniors would take the blame.

The plan worked perfectly—so perfectly, in fact, that the juniors were disqualified from the homecoming parade. I was thrilled! Without the plastic wrap, our float looked terrific, and our greatest competition for the contest was no longer a threat! But my friend Will felt guilty. He, being a better man than I was, went to our school's administration and confessed that we sabotaged our own float. He asked them not to penalize the juniors.

I ended up in Mr. Richardson's office. He was a teacher and advisor known for shooting straight and telling students the truth. In the midst of reprimanding me for organizing and executing such a stupid plan, he said something that changed the way I've thought about myself from that day to this. He said, "Kevin, it's obvious that you have leadership abilities. You can influence people and inspire them with your ideas. The question you have to answer is whether you're going to use those abilities for good or bad. That's up to you."

I still remember that conversation. I had never seen myself as a leader. In my self-perception, I was a somewhat mischievous kid whose goal in life was to do crazy things and not get caught. But Mr. Richardson didn't see a pain in the butt; he saw a young man with potential and was urging me to use it.

In other words, he was telling me I needed to think more deeply about my *positioning*—moving the minds and hearts of people to prompt them to productive action. Mr. Richardson recognized I had leadership abilities, but I had been positioning myself and my message for purposes that weren't helpful to the people around me. With his insight and encouragement, I began to see myself very differently: I could use my talent for good.

Many people perceive positioning as spin and shading the truth, but leaders learn to see it as a necessary tool to unlock and unleash the potential of concepts they need to communicate.

MOVING MINDS AND HEARTS

Leaders are always selling, so positioning isn't a secondary issue. One of the leader's main tasks is to move minds and hearts—those on their team, the rest of the organization, and the customers and clients. For many people, *selling* conjures up sinister motives and the willingness to shade the truth, but we need a better definition. Leaders are communicators who want to persuade, convince, and move

Selling is inherently persuasive, but it's not inherently wrong.

people to a new conviction (or perhaps reinforce an existing one). Every print ad and TV commercial has this goal. I would argue that the leader of every team meeting, every interview, every interaction with an employee, and every connection with the public has the same goal. We're consistently positioning an idea, a strategy, a product, or a service in a way that convinces someone else to buy in. Selling is inherently persuasive, but it's not inherently wrong.

One way to understand leadership is to use the lens of positioning to measure effectiveness. Those who can persuade—from John F.

Kennedy to Martin Luther King, Jr. to Steve Jobs—change the direction of a nation, change the business landscape, and perhaps, change the world.

If we believe our ideas, products, or services will stand on their own and attract attention, we're wrong. When a chef brings bags of groceries into the kitchen, the food has a lot of potential, but it isn't attractive or delicious . . . yet. The chef uses every ounce of her consummate skill to transform those raw materials into dishes that delight guests—and the guests pay enormous amounts of money to enjoy them. Leaders are chefs who transform facts and ideas into something tantalizing that makes people want what we're offering.

I know people who reject this perspective. They're convinced that all marketing is manipulative, and worse, detestable. I must disagree. I've learned from my conversations with them that almost universally they've had bad experiences with leaders who misrepresented the truth and manipulated people with deceptive promises. They recoil from such manipulation, and so do I. Positioning should never be deceptive or manipulative. Rather, it should honestly present the benefits and the costs.

Marketing matters. A friend told me he and another guy went to a bookstore and looked at two books on the same topic. One of them was beautifully written with powerful insights, but the publisher hadn't pushed the book, so it had sold only a few thousand copies. The other book had virtually nothing new to say on the topic, but the publisher had poured a lot of money and creativity into marketing. That book had sold over 100,000 copies. The difference in the impact wasn't the quality of the books; it was due to the skill of how each one was positioned. We could make the same observation about all kinds of products, services, political ideas, strategies, and leadership tools—the ones that are positioned well make the biggest impact, even if they are somewhat inferior.

This principle plays out in organizations every single day. Many leaders conduct team meetings with only a to-do list, and the meeting becomes lifeless and boring. We need to realize that meetings are the beating heart of our organizations, and we need to inject passion, or at least interest, with vision, stories, and regular explanations about how the efforts of each team member makes a difference. That's positioning.

Of course, some leaders use meetings to spin the truth, to convince people on the team that half-truths are the whole truth, and even in the shadow of impending disaster to attempt to assure the team that everything is just fine. One senior vice president told me that when his company was under regulatory pressure, every weekly staff meeting became a dark comedy as the CEO assured the team all was well—a myth everyone first suspected and soon discovered definitely wasn't true. For the first few weeks, they asked hard questions, but only received superficial, glowingly positive answers. After a while, they simply endured those meetings, knowing the ax was going to fall sooner or later. That CEO could have used those months to be honest and enlist the best ideas from those who had a vested interest in the success of the company. Instead, he demoralized them, shattering their trust in him and anything he said.

IN THE RIGHT ORDER

We won't have accurate insights about positioning until we've internalized the perspectives on purpose, priority, people, process, profit, and power. If we are seriously trying to get those things right, we'll recognize the difference between necessary positioning and manipulative spin. We won't conclude on one hand that positioning is wrong or on the other that employing any means of convincing people is acceptable. Our communication must have a powerful blend of honesty and hope—speaking the truth in a way that convinces people and moves them to action.

> **Our communication must have a powerful blend of honesty and hope—speaking the truth in a way that convinces people and moves them to action.**

Positioning is a skill all effective leaders must cultivate. It's not secondary to our role; it's the ability to express what's most important. If you're not applying the principles of the first six chapters, don't even concern yourself with positioning. First go back and read those chapters again. They are the heart and soul of leadership, the motives and methods that shape our direction. Only when those concepts are operative are we ready to use every communication skill we have to inspire people to join us.

Do people around us know what's in our hearts? Can they tell whether we're communicating the truth or manipulating them? To be honest, some are pretty clueless and will believe us no matter what we say, but many others see through our words into our souls. Every leader uses words, but communication also has a nonverbal subtext. The message coming out of the CEO's mouth may be, "We're a great company, and you're a great team." Perceptive listeners, however, may pick up a hidden message that the CEO doesn't intend to communicate: "And since I'm your leader, I deserve all the credit!" People who see below the surface often detect a message the leader doesn't literally *say*.

Of course, some people are cynical and see a selfish subtext in a leader's communication even when he or she is sincere. We need to be careful not to make negative assumptions about motives, but we also need to be perceptive. Virtually none of us can recognize selfish sub-texts in our own nonverbal communication. We're blind to them, so we need someone else to tell us if our verbal message is clouded by a nonverbal signal that contradicts our words. That is why it's essential for us to first wade through the previous chapters, clarify our purpose, and sharpen our views on the other important leadership issues before we attempt to analyze our communication with our teams, the rest of our employees, and the public.

PRINCIPLES OF POSITIONING

In leading our team, consulting with leaders, and speaking to groups, I've learned some valuable lessons about positioning:

Speak to people; don't just use talking points.

No matter who is in front of me, one person or thousands, I need to understand their purpose and tailor my points to help them fulfill it. It's not my job to change their purpose—perhaps to help them clarify it, but not to change it to suit me. I first need to understand what matters most to them before I can shape my message to address it.

Invest time in preparation.

As I have mentioned, some leaders walk into a staff meeting with little more than a to-do list. Their agenda is to go over it point by point. I'm not against lists of things that need to be covered, but it's important for leaders to move hearts, not just pens, keyboards, and bodies. Even for the most mundane of topics, leaders need to consider ahead of time how to frame the tasks so everyone sees the bigger picture—how those tasks are part of the process of fulfilling the purpose, what benefit it will make in others' lives, and what a difference it makes to the leader.

Great leaders are also great storytellers. They know that a story—about a team member, a client, or anyone who has done something inspiring—is one of the most effective ways to move a person's heart. It takes time to craft a good story, or perhaps to find one, but it's worth its weight in gold.

Know your audience.

What are the dreams of the people who hear or read your message? What difficulties have they been going through? What revs their creative engines? What erodes their motivation? What level in the organization are you talking to?

Everybody needs to connect their purpose with the priority of the day, so top executives use different stresses and responsibilities with mid-level managers and frontline employees. This, however, is where some people become cynical. They hear us tailor our message for different audiences, and they assume we're trying to manipulate them. But smart leaders understand the differences between audiences and then nuance the same truth so each group can hear it, grasp the implications, and take appropriate action. That's not spin; that's positioning. Communication is what's heard, not what's said, so we need to understand how each audience hears us.

Communication is what's heard, not what's said.

For each group and team, and perhaps for each person, understand the level of receptivity or resistance to your message. How familiar they are with the concept or product? How much information do they need to respond? How much time do they need to process the information? How much do they trust the leadership as they approach a new threat or challenge? What do they stand to gain by responding positively? Many leaders assume their teams intuitively know the answers to these questions, but it might be constructive to think more about them . . . before the next meeting.

Leverage emotion.

God has made us complex emotional beings. We're not robots. We care, we dread, we desire. When we're under the most pressure, we especially need to communicate with empathy and clarity. When I lead a team meeting or speak to a group, I try to use Winston Churchill's method: start strong, use simple language, include vivid imagery, communicate a single theme, and end with an emotional call to action. The flow of a good talk is more like the gradual anticipation and exhilarating thrill of a ride on a roller coaster instead of the flat constancy of a merry-go-round.

Make it memorable.

Complex concepts are very difficult for employees or customers to grasp. They may sound good in the boardroom, but they quickly lose their punch a few minutes after the meeting is over. Leaders need to craft their messages so everyone can repeat them.

Andy Stanley insists, "It is better to have a vision statement that is incomplete and memorable than to have one that is complete and forgettable." A vision being memorable makes it portable, which enables others to remember and repeat it. He explains,

> "People don't remember or embrace paragraphs. They remember and embrace sentences. As theologian Howard Hendricks said, 'If it's a mist in the pulpit, it's a fog in the pew.' If your vision is unclear to you, it will never be clear to the people in

your organization. For your vision to stick, you may need to clarify or simplify it."[46]

Make sure people understand the problem to be solved.

Too often, we jump to the solution too soon because we assume people understand the problem. Sometimes the problem is readily apparent, but even then, it doesn't hurt for the listener(s) to grasp the gravity of why the problem needs to be solved. I recommend leaders take time to articulate the harm the problem is creating, which then enables them to describe the importance of finding the right solution. Only then can the person or the team respond wholeheartedly to the leader's call to action.

Articulate the payoff.

You've talked about the what and the how, and you've asked them to respond. Before ending the meeting, the talk, or the memo, be sure to paint a picture of how each person's buy-in of the concepts and processes will make a difference. Leave them with the understanding that what they'll do will have tangible benefits—for themselves, for the team, and for the people they serve. Describing the benefits of the buy-in is important in every relationship—with spouses, children, friends, teams, vendors, and customers.

Evaluate your marketing.

As you present your company to the public and offer your products and services, the same principles of truth and hope apply. With integrity, describe the benefits you offer. Your marketing message includes many of the same characteristics of your internal positioning: take care to prepare the message, speak the truth, tell a story that connects with hearts, articulate a problem and show how to solve it, and keep it simple. Joe Chernov, vice president of marketing at InsightSquared, quipped, "Good marketing makes the company look smart. Great marketing makes the customer feel smart."[47] That's how you know you've connected with people.

Understand the difference between insights and instincts.

Data is important, but great leaders have another level of understanding: they have a sixth sense of reliable instincts. I vividly remember making a presentation to one of our clients. I was confident because our staff had done a lot of research and we had crafted it with graphs to impress him. When I finished, I felt confident I'd hit a home run, but he said something that surprised me: "Kevin, I love all of this stuff. It's really good. Just don't become too focused on it. Remember why we wanted to work with you in the first place. We didn't hire you for your insights; we hired you for your instincts."

After thinking long and hard about his comment, I realized he was right. All good leaders have insights based on accurate data, but the best leaders have strong instincts about how to use that information. I've drawn several conclusions about the necessity of instincts:

- Insights help you identify a target audience; instincts help you connect with that audience in an authentic way. Plenty of tech companies produce incredible products, but Apple consistently comes out on top because they've connected so well to their customers' wants and needs. They know their audience appreciates accessible, easy-to-use technology, so they appeal to them with outstanding products and simple, attractive marketing. The instincts of Steve Jobs and other leaders at Apple have propelled them to the top of their industry.

- Insights gleaned from research tell you what people want; instincts help you design what people really need. Steve Jobs remarked,

"If Henry Ford had asked people what they wanted, they would have said faster horses." Ford had the instinct to design a form of transportation that was beyond what people could even imagine.

- Insights based on data tell you where you're going; instincts show you the path to get there. Research is necessary, but it's not enough. Leaders need the sensitivity, the savvy, the perception to see what others can't see so they can go where no one has gone before.

Insights coupled with instincts lead to innovation that changes the world.

The conversation with my client challenged me to look beyond raw numbers—even very helpful raw numbers— and combine those insights with the instincts that I know are valuable. Insights coupled with instincts lead to innovation that changes the world.

POSITIONING PEOPLE

Titles aren't necessary to make a powerful impact on a team. More important is positioning team members in the right places, or as Jim Collins would say, "Get the right people on the bus in the right seats."[48]

I led a team a few years ago, and most of the people were eager to advance the corporate purpose. But one guy apparently saw it as his mission in life to contaminate every meeting and crush every vision. He was brilliantly passive-aggressive, laughing as he cut me and my ideas to shreds, and avoiding any responsibility for his words by insisting, "This is what everybody thinks," or "Hey, I was just kidding." The truth is that no one on the team wanted to be the target of his attacks, so they seldom disagreed with him.

His negativity became contagious, and I didn't recognize the problem soon enough. The damage was severe. In some of the most important conversations with the team about our direction, he convinced enough of the others that my ideas were at least deficient, if not completely stupid. He moved hearts and minds, but not in a good way! I spent more time with him than anyone else, trying to convince him to see the benefits of my ideas, but it was a colossal waste of time. I realized later that he relished all the attention I was giving him, and he had me wrapped around his finger. I was too far too slow to see the game he was playing.

In stark contrast, I've seen people earn a position of influence, not because they were given a title, but because people grew to respect their character. A few years ago, a woman on our team had a profoundly positive impact on all the rest of us. She had a lot of relational equity with everyone because we knew she cared deeply about us. She remembered birthdays and made them special, she listened while others talked, and she freely gave her honest opinions. Instead of jumping in to offer her input, she often first asked for clarification: "Tell me more about that." Her love for people came "with no strings attached": she wasn't trying to gain favor or manipulate anyone. She seldom originated new ideas or new processes, but those who did looked for her response. If she was confused, they felt safe voicing their concerns. If she jumped on board, they tried to see the benefits she saw. Though she didn't have a position of leadership, she was the thermostat that maintained a pleasant environment in the room—always making it more comfortable and productive. I soon realized that if I was going to present a new idea to our team, it was wise for me to run it by her first. Sometimes she instantly bought it, but plenty of times, her questions shaped my idea or my form of communication. I used her influence on the team to help me position my message so it could be clearer and more effective.

THE PRIVILEGE OF PLATFORM

I've had the privilege of being around leaders who exemplify the best hearts and best practices of good positioning. After a meeting or a talk, people consistently come away with a refreshed sense of vision and renewed energy to fulfill the company's purpose. Some might assume their positive response was "natural," but I know better. Those leaders had worked hard to know what inflames passion and what dampens excitement. They had listened to people and determined how to craft their message so it would be clearly understood and relevant. They're often painfully honest, even about their own failures, which gives them tremendous credibility with the people who hear them. They're using their platform of leadership to have a very positive impact on others.

I've also seen the other extreme. A CEO once told me about a nationally known marketing expert: "I know he's a huge success and his books sell, but his readers don't know him like I do. His staff and those close to him know he's a phony. He's all smiles on stage, but he's rude to a lot of people in private. He only cares about one person: himself." I knew what this CEO said was true because I'd experienced the same treatment from the marketing expert. I assumed he was just having a bad day, so I had given him the benefit of the doubt. But since then, I heard many more people tell similar, and similarly painful, stories about their interactions with him. No matter how brilliant he has been at marketing his insights to the public, he is lousy at positioning himself and his message to the people close to him.

Leadership is a position of honor. People look to their leaders for wisdom and direction, but the role comes with an implied warning. Jesus said, "Everyone to whom much was given, of him much will be required, and from him to whom they entrusted much, they will demand the more."[49] Leaders, because of their influence, are necessarily under more scrutiny than others in the organization—from their teams, their shareholders, and their clients and customers.

Those on the outside may look at us and admire our positive qualities, but those who are closest to us see plenty of flaws. The old saying is, "No man is a hero to his valet." I might update it a bit: "No person is flawless to best friends." The point is that even the most powerful, talented, and popular people inevitably disappoint those who know them well and see them in their unguarded moments.

Positioning is important in all types of work. When we look through the lens of leadership and view positioning correctly, we increase our potential to influence others. The words we use matter, and those words are most effective when what we *do* matches what we *say*. That's where the magic happens—when what we sell is coupled with a posture of servant leadership.

> *The difference between the right word and the almost right word*
> *is the difference between lightning and a lightning bug.*
> —*Mark Twain*

TAKE A LOOK . . .

1. How would you define and describe *positioning*?

2. In leadership, when is positioning good and right and positive? When is it deceptive and manipulative? Give some examples for both cases.

3. What are some reasons leaders don't prepare for meetings well enough to capture the hearts of the people in the room? What do they lose by their lack of preparation? What would they gain by preparing better?

4. How important are stories in a business meeting? Who do you know who tells great stories? What can you learn from that person?

5. Andy Stanley talked about the importance of leaders simplifying their vision: "If it's not memorable, it's not portable." How can you improve on making your vision (or stated purpose or today's priority) more memorable?

6. What is your biggest strength in positioning yourself and your message to your team? What needs to improve? What would your closest friend say are your strengths and weaknesses in positioning? What are you going to do about it?

CHAPTER 8
PROXIMITY

Most people believe vulnerability is weakness. But really vulnerability is
courage. We must ask ourselves . . . are we willing to show up and be seen.
—*Brené Brown*

The inverse relationship between position and proximity creates one of the greatest difficulties in leadership: the higher leaders climb in an organization, the greater the distance between them and the frontline team and customers. We spend our time and energies designing solutions for people who can become increasingly distant from us. To add to the problem, companies often invest more than ninety percent of professional development dollars in the top five percent of the organizational chart even though the people who have the biggest impact on customer experience are frontline employees. Top executives might get a personal coach, the executive team goes on a lavish annual retreat, and mid-level managers are sent to a conference, while the employees who interact with customers may be lucky to get a company handbook.

This disparity of investments can be justified to some extent. After all, the top-level executives make decisions that affect the maintenance and growth of the company, if not its very survival. They also make a disproportionate share of salaries, so it seems to make sense to provide them the finest resources to keep them sharp. Mid-level managers and department heads make important decisions as well, but not earthshaking ones. People at the bottom of the organizational chart are more transient, and they are considered replaceable, if not expendable.

To many executives, it doesn't make sense to invest a lot to train those people. After all, they may leave and take their new skills to a competitor who pays them a few dollars more!

This pattern is evident throughout the business and nonprofit world: in local restaurants, multinational companies, grocery stores, retail chains, airlines, tech companies, and every other enterprise. Generally, customers interact with a person on the lowest level of the organizational chart. Meanwhile, as I've pointed out, two corollary problems make things worse: top executives don't invest much to equip the people who connect directly with customers, and the executives themselves tend to lose touch with the day-to-day problems and opportunities of workers who serve customers and clients.

Many people perceive that by climbing the corporate ladder, distance is deserved, but leaders need to acknowledge the importance of communicating care by maintaining contact.

SURPRISE CONNECTIONS

It can be enlightening to watch a few episodes of *Undercover Boss*. The premise of the show is that the CEO or president of a company puts on a disguise and becomes "the new employee" at an entry-level position. He or she may become a driver, work in a call center, stock shelves, or clean rooms. The program depicts, with pathos and humor, the benefits of a common management theory: Management by Wandering Around (MBWA). The episodes evoke laughter and groans as we see the boss sometimes fail to do even the simplest tasks, or at least struggle to get them done.

In an article titled, "5 Lessons from Undercover Boss," Mark Kolakowski observes, "The CEOs and other executives who go undercover are astonishingly out-of-touch with how their companies actually run. This is particularly amazing with respect to those entrepreneurs, increasingly featured on the show, who purportedly built their firms from scratch, and from the bottom up."[50]

The bosses are shocked to discover the low pay, the working conditions, and the lack of training. Almost without exception, by the end of the episode, the boss has far greater appreciation for the people who are performing essential but often overlooked jobs for the company. That doesn't mean CEOs need to be proficient in every menial job, but they do need to know enough of that world to understand the complexity of the most important interactions in the life of the company.

When leaders aren't close enough to the problem or the crucial connection between frontline workers and customers, they can make any or all of three mistakes: (1) they misidentify the problem; (2) they find inadequate solutions; or (3) they miscommunicate the right solutions. All of these mistakes produce frustration in the employees and customers, and they erode trust on both sides of that conversation. Leaders need to be "close to the ground" instead of cloistering in the corporate office, especially as they construct training programs for staff, solutions for customers, and processes that enhance the important conversations between employees and customers—even if those processes require more effort from executives and managers.

Where does the magic happen in a company? In the boardroom? The executive team meeting? In management meetings, or training events, or sales meetings? All these gatherings are important, but the *most* crucial event is the interaction between an employee and a customer—even in B2B sales. Our job—not our only job, but a very important one—is to fully support the people we lead in these interactions. However, we can't serve them if we don't know them. Nor can we support them if we aren't immersed in their challenges and if we don't listen to their suggestions. We can't improve customer service from the corner office. The annual survey may provide some statistics, but it doesn't produce deeper insights, understanding, and trust. Big problems aren't solved at a distance, and big opportunities won't be realized if we don't respect the magic of employees connecting with customers.

LURED AWAY

None of us intend to become detached. We don't make being distant a personal goal. We have no plans to lose proximity. Most likely, when we were promoted we were acutely aware of the hopes and challenges of the people around us . . . because we experienced those same desires and dreads. Over time, however, the new role refocused our attention upward. We grew more in touch with the goals set by the executive team (or the next level up) and gradually lost our sensitivity to the people now below us on the organizational chart. It's not intentional, but leaders often drift that way and will continue to do so if they don't make a shift in the other direction.

Sometimes the distance is created by ego: rising leaders presume they're better, smarter, more skilled, more connected, and more valuable than the people they've passed on the ladder of success. They want to be identified with the up-and-comers, not the people still on the lowest rung. Because they have more responsibility and more pressure in the new role, they justify giving less attention to people down the chain of command. Whatever the reason, the lack of proximity is a big problem for many leaders.

Staying in touch requires time, intentionality, and empathy. For many, that's one thing too many on their to-do list, so they keep a "healthy distance" from the lower echelons. The distance relieves their immediate discomfort, but it creates an organizational numbness. Effective problem-solving requires leaders to be close to the most important connections in corporate life. In many other areas, we need to zoom out to get a better perspective, but this is an area where we necessarily need to zoom in. When leaders are closer to the workers who attend to those outside the organization, they'll have more empathy and understanding, they'll build more trust, and they'll make better decisions.

Let me throw another rock in the pond and create a few ripples: The solution to a leader's isolation isn't just to show up from time to time to address a problem at the call center (or wherever the organization's most basic conversation takes place). Proximity entails really getting to know workers to assure them *they* are valuable, not just that *what they do* is valuable to the company's bottom line. Do you think frontline employees can tell the difference? You bet they can! They're glad to see a top executive show up to pat them on the back and tell them they're doing a great job, but it means so much more when the boss stops to ask about the person's spouse or child . . . and listens. Yes, this level of involvement takes time, but the health of an organization's culture is based on trust, and trust takes more than time—it requires empathy.

> **Proximity entails really getting to know workers to assure them *they* are valuable, not just that *what they do* is valuable to the company's bottom line.**

THE POWER OF CARING

Doug Dietz is an industrial designer who oversees the manufacture and installation of magnetic resonance imaging machines (MRIs). In a TEDx talk, he described one day when he had finished the installation of one of his machines. He was proud of his work and ready to leave when a couple walked in with their little girl who was about seven years old. She obviously had a severe health problem, and her doctors had ordered a scan to find out what was going on in her body. When the girl came into the room, she was terrified. Her father leaned over and tried to reassure her. He whispered, "Just like we talked about, be brave."

For the first time, Dietz saw the room and the machine through a child's eyes. He had been so proud of his creation because it was technically advanced and fully functional. Now, through this new lens, he saw a monstrosity. Everything about the room was menacing, especially for a little girl who didn't feel very good anyway. It was huge and drab and forbidding. The walls, the floor, and the machine itself were all a dull beige.

Dietz began a very personal journey to create an environment where children wouldn't be afraid of an MRI. He created elaborate settings: jungles and pirate ships, with the patient positioned in a machine shaped and painted like a canoe or other fanciful scenes. He even laid out a path of rocks starting down the hall outside the room, a path to indicate that this was going to be a pleasant adventure instead of a terrifying threat.

MRIs are loud and require patients to be still for a long time. After a tech put a child in one of the machines painted to look like a boat on the ocean, Dietz told the child, "If you hold really still, the fish will start jumping over you." The child was still and silent for the entire time in the machine. Previously about eighty percent of children had to be sedated for the procedure, but with the new designs, fewer than one percent now require sedation.

The impact of Dietz's care and imagination go far beyond the child's time spent in the machine. He said that the influence of his new machines continues in conversations on the way home. The parents, who are already worried and stressed about the child's illness, no longer need to comfort a traumatized child. Instead, they can laugh and talk about the wonder of the rock path, the pirate ship, the jumping fish, the canoe, the bright blue sky, and the kind people who cared for them.

Doug Dietz defines empathy as "imaginative projection of one's own consciousness on another person." That's what moved him when the little girl and her parents walked into the hospital room that day. At that moment, he put himself in the little girl's shoes, her fears became his fears, and he did something to make life better for her and other children like her.[51]

In 2017, the power suddenly went out at the Atlanta Airport. Everything ground to a halt at the busiest airport in the country. (Later, they discovered a rat had gnawed through a cable. Thousands of people were stopped by a single pest, but that's an illustration for another time.)

A few hours later, the news carried pictures of Dan Cathy, the CEO of Chick-fil-A, passing out chicken sandwiches to thousands of people at the airport. It was a wonderful example of an executive stepping into the nitty-gritty of a problem to show compassion.

Meanwhile an equally positive example was taking place nearby, although it didn't get as much press. Ed Bastian, the CEO of Delta Air Lines, went to the airport, too. He waded into the chaos, answering questions and providing assurance. Many Delta executives even went out to the tarmac to help move luggage more quickly. These efforts, though, didn't result in all sweetness and light. Several frustrated, irate, would-be passengers took out their anger on the CEO. Even though they unfairly blamed him for the problem when they should have blamed a rat, he didn't shield himself from their venting. He put himself in their shoes and showed empathy for their plight.

Leaders often hear the mantra: "You need to work *on* the business, not *in* the business." I believe that's basically true, but not universally so. I certainly need to work on the business in planning and organizing, but

I also need to show up enough in every sphere of our organization so I can appreciate all the people who work here and their important roles. I don't need to know exactly how they do every single task, but I want them to know that I "get it." They want me to be aware of what helps them feel great about themselves and what they do, and what gets in the way and frustrates them. I can't know those things if I don't know them, and I can't know them unless I spend time with them.

Of course, there are always time limits. As an organization grows, more layers of leadership form, and leaders must become more intentional about connecting with people. When we began our first leader academy, we piloted the program in three schools. I could easily meet with the manager in the local business that sponsored the program and get to know the key people at each school. Today, we're in 900 schools in more than forty states, so it's impossible for me to maintain a personal connection with people who represent each of those businesses and schools. It would be easy for me to think, *We've grown too large for me to be involved at the local level any longer,* but that's not my conclusion. I have become more selective about the places where I get more deeply involved, but I'm committed to always—always—be involved with the people on the front lines of our organization. I need to hear their hopes and fears, and they need to know that I care.

As an example, we deploy a video curriculum to conduct and scale our training across the country. I am one of the featured speakers, so I occasionally sit in when one of the videos is shown to see how people receive the message. At times I have been shocked to realize the video was a bomb. What was I thinking? It made perfect sense when I wrote the script and when we filmed it in the studio. I thought the message was clear and powerful and life-changing, but it left people— even me—feeling confused. If I hadn't taken the time to sit alongside the participants, I wouldn't have seen the painful truth. (My staff had often told me it wasn't clear, but I didn't listen.) Showing up to be part of an event or a process as "a fly on the wall" is often an eye-opening experience.

In terms of leadership philosophies, I am a proponent of the teaching of Stanford University's Design School. Their methodology is called "design thinking," which is a process to create innovative solutions. Elizabeth, one of the leaders on our team, is a huge champion of this methodology and challenges us to use it as we develop new programs and experiences. One of the hallmarks of this process is the need for empathy: understanding the critical needs of those the company serves. It's easy to assume we already know what others want and need, but too often, we're a little off base, and sometimes we're dead wrong.

In a *Forbes* article, Roger Dooley describes the dangers of confirmation bias—interpreting research and feedback only through a lens that reinforces our preconceived conclusions. Leaders have risen to their positions by being sharp, insightful, and very often right. They have confidence in their perceptions . . . sometimes too much confidence. Dooley relates his experience with a CEO who was looking through a faulty lens:

> "The CEO had achieved past success in selling commodity products at higher prices by differentiating with service and quality. He was convinced that the same strategy would work in our market, too. When a customer survey showed that 'price' ranked behind multiple other factors in importance, nobody asked, 'Why?' Nobody suggested that the question be asked in a different way, or that this surprising result be explored in more detail. Instead, confirmation bias kicked in. The survey was viewed as proof that price wasn't all that important, and

that a differentiation strategy would allow at least a modest price premium over less skilled competitors."

The result of the CEO's unwillingness to try harder to grasp the implications of the research was a decline in sales. He failed to ask follow-up questions to understand their customers. Dooley recommends, "If you are doing market research or analyzing customer feedback, be very careful to look for alternate ways of interpreting the information. Look for dissenting voices within your team or company when you analyze customer data, and don't be afraid to follow up on important data points."[52]

A leader's tunnel vision also creates problems on a team. I know because I've been guilty too many times. I've walked into a meeting with my agenda firmly implanted in my mind. My gaze was riveted on communicating my vision and infusing my team with passion to accomplish it. That worked just fine most of the time, but occasionally I failed to notice someone on the team who was preoccupied with a problem—a sick child, a spouse who just lost a job, a financial setback, or another serious issue. I put my head down and plowed through the meeting, more than a little peeved the team member wasn't as attentive or excited as I would have liked. If I'd been more observant, I could have taken a couple of minutes to ask a question, communicate care, and improve the trust between us. My oblivion and negative assumptions had the opposite effect, which often required additional conversations and a lot more time to rectify. But I'm learning.

CREATING THE ENVIRONMENT

Some people, as we've seen, are temperamentally nice, but that's not the same as being truly empathetic. Those who are sweet seldom ask hard questions, so they rarely uncover the hidden complexities of problems. It takes more than being nice to create a culture of empathy, one that enables a team to connect with one another as well as their customers. Here are some suggestions:

Carve out time to be with people.

Visit the call center, meet with the people in shipping, and go to lunch with people out in the field who are providing services to customers. While you're there, don't make it a show. They'll wonder why you're there. Are you assuming they're messing up and you're going to drop the hammer? Are you just checking them off your list that proves you're connected, or do you really care about them, their hopes and dreams, and their frustrations with the job? Your presence matters, as does your nonverbal message. Empathy doesn't always result from research, data, or a sophisticated feedback loop. It often requires physical proximity. You don't need to spend half your time running a cash register or mopping floors, but you do need to spend enough time so that you genuinely grasp what's going on in the lives of employees throughout the organizational chart.

> **It takes more than being nice to create a culture of empathy, one that enables a team to connect with one another as well as their customers.**

Consider being an undercover boss, or at least an undercover customer.

If your company is large enough, show up where the frontline people have no idea who you are and see how it feels to be either a new hire or a random customer. Just keep in mind that a single experience probably doesn't paint the whole picture. It's only one brushstroke on the canvas of insight and empathy you're creating.

A popular pastor sometimes shows up at one of the church's satellite campuses and becomes just one of the crowd. He wants to sense what it feels like to be someone who attends the church for the first time. I'm pretty sure many of the people in the church recognize this pastor when he sits next to them, but I'm reasonably certain the frustrated people in the dark in the Atlanta airport had no idea the man answering their questions and hauling luggage was a senior-level executive of one of the major airlines.

Assume you have confirmation bias.

We all do. Thanks to our family backgrounds, our training, our personalities, and our experiences, we've put on glasses through which we see the world—but any single set of lenses is necessarily limited. It's not a character flaw to have confirmation bias, but it's detrimental to refuse to admit it. When we admit the possibility that our perception may not provide the full story, we become open to alternate, and maybe even competing, perspectives that will probably feel uncomfortable, at least for a while. But our openness can lead to more creativity, more enthusiasm, and better service for our customers . . . which translates into more revenues for the company.

Put proximity into your regular schedule . . . and other leaders' schedules.

If a leader's connection with frontline employees and customers is "one and done," it won't create a culture of empathy, and it may actually erode trust if employees assume the leader doesn't really care after all. On some regular basis—weekly, monthly, or no less than quarterly—schedule time to leave the office and go into the field. Depending on the company's size and the nature of the business, you may only need a couple of hours, or you may need a full day so you have time to have meaningful conversations with enough people. If connecting with people isn't on your schedule, empathy won't become part of your company's culture.

In addition, executives need to require the people on their teams and all managers to regularly get out of their offices, too. They will probably have different insights than the CEO, and together, the team can serve more effectively. To create a culture of empathy, many people at all levels of leadership and management need to invest time in connecting with others. Make this part of their performance review. Yes, it's that important.

> **If connecting with people isn't on your schedule, empathy won't become part of your company's culture.**

Good leaders blend vision and organizational skills to move their company forward, but great leaders add the intangible asset of empathy, which becomes the glue that holds people together so they care about one another as they work to achieve the corporate purpose. Empathy, that deepest and most profound connection with another person, never happens at a distance. It requires proximity, closeness, so we see what others see, feel what others feel, and are moved by their hopes and fears.

Empathy is about standing in someone else's shoes, feeling with his or her heart, seeing with his or her eyes. Not only is empathy hard to outsource and automate, but it makes the world a better place.
—Daniel H. Pink

TAKE A LOOK . . .

1. Why do you think it makes sense to many corporate executives to spend ninety percent of their professional development dollars on the top five percent of their employees? After reading this chapter, how would you allocate development dollars? Explain your answer.

2. How would you define and describe empathy? Who is at least one person you know who exemplifies this quality?

3. What are some common excuses leaders use to remain in their offices instead of connecting with frontline employees and customers?

4.   What are some reasons confirmation bias feels so right? What can you do to recognize it in yourself and your team members?

5.   What do you think moved Doug Dietz, and what is the magic in *Undercover Boss*?

6.   As you look at the practical suggestions at the end of the chapter, what specific steps will you take to create opportunities for proximity, which can produce more empathy?

CHAPTER 9
PROGRESS

We can each define ambition and progress for ourselves. The goal is to work toward a world where expectations are not set by the stereotypes that hold us back, but by our personal passion, talents and interests.
—Sheryl Sandberg

At a conference where I was speaking, a woman asked to talk to me. I could tell she wanted more than to say, "Hello" or "I liked your talk." After the audience had dispersed, she almost whispered, "I'd like your perspective about how to live and work in our company." I asked her to tell me what was going on. She explained, "Almost like clockwork, the senior executives launch a major reorganization of the company. It may be the organizational chart, the reporting guidelines, the communication between departments, or something else."

I asked, "So . . . what's wrong with those changes?"

Her eyes narrowed with obvious frustration as she told me, "They always *say* they're instituting changes, but nothing ever really changes. We're not more productive, we're not selling more products, we're not communicating any better with each other, and we're not serving our customers any more effectively. It's driving me crazy to spend so much time adjusting to changes that don't make a difference."

Months later, I had a conversation with a senior executive in a different company. He described a similar problem, but he had a solution. He told me, "Our company is all about change. We've done research on the changes in the work styles and values of millennials, the rapid changes in technology, advances in hiring methodology, and a dozen other studies. Our company is dedicated to embrace change so we remain relevant."

It all sounded good to me, but I could tell he was arriving at a different conclusion than the stock line about the necessity of change. He summarized his viewpoint: "We keep talking about *change*, but we really need to be talking about *progress*. We need to remember that all progress involves change, but not all change is progress."

Some leaders, like those leading the company of the woman I met at the conference, seem to value change for its own sake. Maybe they imagine they're throwing spaghetti at the wall, hoping that at least one noodle will stick. But I don't think that's it. All the leaders I know are convinced their new structure, new process, new product design, or new reporting system will produce substantive results—real progress. They're surprised when it doesn't, so they try the next new idea. Quite often, the "next new idea" comes from a conference, an article in a respected journal, or a report from their industry. Those leaders too quickly jump on the bandwagon without careful analysis of how the process worked in the author's or speaker's company, and how the principles may (or may not) apply in their own. This *herd effect* is rampant in American business today.

But the other side of the spectrum is also prevalent: *the igloo effect*. Some leaders have tried one new idea too many and feel burned, or maybe had their latest idea bomb so badly they became gun-shy about trying anything else. They've had enough, so they're content to leave well enough alone. They may tinker with the edges, fine-tuning the system, but they aren't going to try anything bold and innovative. For them, change represents too much of a threat, and their resistance causes them to forfeit opportunities for real progress.

Change isn't the real issue. We need a new calculus to measure the value of anything new we implement, and that calculus is progress: better outcomes for our customers, clients, and employees. If change doesn't produce improvements, it's worthless, and in fact, counterproductive because it erodes employees' confidence in their leaders.

Many people believe that progress happens naturally because it's part of the plan, but leaders learn to see that growth isn't guaranteed and only happens with intentional focus.

Several business experts have recently begun to advocate a fundamental shift in what is measured: outcomes instead of outputs. Instead of looking primarily at the performance of each department, such as customer service, they prefer a qualitative analysis of the *impact* of the performance: customer satisfaction, and indeed, customer delight. In a *Forbes* article, Steve Denning explains that "shareholder capitalism," measuring the financial benefits of changing the system to produce more profits, is over. "Making money and corporate survival now depend not merely on satisfying customers but on delighting them." He elaborates:

> "It's not enough just to *talk* about delighting customers and shifting from outputs to outcomes. To manage the new bottom line of business, we have to *measure* it. Thus, traditional management was right to insist on the importance of measurement. The trouble was that they were measuring the wrong things. They were measuring *outputs*, rather than *outcomes*. By counting outputs, i.e. things, they were missing what is really driving the business, the outcomes with customers."[53]

Denning recommends that business leaders measure customer delight and focus organizational change on enhancing that delight through better service, better products, time, and a vital presence on social media. Through this grid, prospective changes—in products, services, policies, and processes—undergo rigorous analysis to determine if they promise to delight customers. The same principle can be applied internally, measuring outcomes instead of outputs related to employee satisfaction, performance, and yes, delight in working at the company.

MANAGING EXPECTATIONS

Delight is relative: a person's experience of satisfaction is dependent on expectations. One of our jobs as leaders is to manage the expectations of our employees and customers. A few years ago, the ADDO Institute took leaders to remote parts of the world where they could be immersed in another culture and serve underprivileged people. On virtually every trip, we explained that living conditions would be difficult, but the interactions with people would be incredibly fulfilling. We did a great job preparing people for these trips . . . except for one time.

To prepare for one of the excursions, Garrett and I went to Cuba for the first time and had an amazing experience. It's tough to put into words how fascinating it was—Cuba is only ninety miles from the United States, but in many ways, it's stuck in the 1950s. I loved the experience and we were eager to take others back to Cuba with us.

After working through the licensing process to travel legally into Cuba, we decided to create an "ADDO Ambassador trip." Our first group of people went in 2011, and to our surprise, most of them were disillusioned and disappointed.

They agreed that Cuba was interesting, but they were unimpressed with the hotel because it was old. Communication with friends and family back home was nearly impossible because access to Wi-Fi was limited—it was incredibly expensive and worked at the speed of dial-up. Our schedule changed constantly and required flexibility as the itinerary shifted from day to day.

It became clear that participants enjoyed the culture and experience; most of the dissatisfaction was the result of unmet expectations. Our organization hadn't taken the time to lay out clear expectations for the trip.

Rather than give up hope that we could make this work, we devised a new plan. The next time we planned a trip to Cuba, we created a flyer appropriately titled, "Is Cuba Right for You? *Maybe.*" In the brochure we explained that Cuba is a unique cultural experience, and that it wouldn't be like going on a typical Caribbean vacation. We made it clear that participants would not be staying at an all-inclusive island resort, but instead would be immersed in the culture of the Cuban people, necessitating a slower pace of life and requiring them to be flexible. We explained that Cuba is an adventure, full of fascinating, unexpected, and often challenging experiences. In a tongue-in-cheek way, we suggested if someone was looking for an easy trip, they should try Europe.

The result? The next trip was amazing! After laying out those clear expectations, our group loved the trip. The hotel still hadn't been updated. Communication remained a problem with limited access to Wi-Fi. Our schedule shifted and changed as before. Yet because the expectations had been set, the group was prepared, and they loved it. The vast difference in perspectives between the two groups, from disappointed to delighted, was completely due to the expectations our organization set for them.

Here's the point: Satisfaction with an experience is largely dependent on expectations being met or exceeded. This principle applies in every aspect of corporate and personal life, and it works both ways:

- If we tell our staff a new process will be a breeze, but it turns out to be a hassle, they'll complain. But if we tell them there will be a period of adjustment and welcome their input, the change will go more smoothly.

- If we tell a new hire the company has the most positive culture in the corporate world, the person will almost undoubtedly be assigned to work near one of the only negative people in the office. But if we admit that there are all kinds of people on staff, the new person won't be as surprised when a difficult coworker creates a few headaches.

- If a restaurant tells me the wait for a table will be forty-five minutes but they call my name in twenty, I feel like I've just picked up a "Get out of jail free!" card.

- When someone we love won't answer the phone or return a text, we feel frustrated and maybe angry.

- If a hotel for a honeymoon or anniversary isn't as nice as expected, we're disappointed . . . especially if we're the one who booked it. But if it's better than expected, the delight is multiplied.

- If your website is easy to use and completely functional (even better than the competition), your visitors and customers will be thrilled. But if they can't find the right page, the site freezes, or if the "buy" function doesn't work correctly, they may quickly find someone else to sell them a similar product.

When I'm visiting a city and someone tells me a restaurant is "the greatest in town," I've learned to be at least a bit skeptical. And I grimace when I'm speaking and the person introducing me tells the audience,

"Kevin is the best speaker I've ever heard!" No matter how good my speech may be, I can seldom rise to those lofty expectations.

Many leaders tend to oversell. Lofty promises may have some benefits on the front end, but they usually lead to the erosion of credibility. Progress in providing customer and employee delight is all about managing their expectations. Do it well, and you win. Do it poorly, and it'll cost more than you want to lose. If the purpose is compelling and the expectations are realistic, people on our teams are much more willing to suffer through growing pains to make progress in fulfilling the purpose.

Don't make changes just because other companies do; avoid the herd effect. Care about more than mere change. Yet don't be afraid to make changes because you've failed in the past, so you also avoid the igloo effect. Pursue genuine progress and be willing to make some waves to get there. Don't overpromise and become immobilized. Purpose inspires people to dream, but providing a realistic path to get there gives them patience and persistence in the process.

Purpose inspires people to dream, but providing a realistic path to get there gives them patience and persistence in the process.

THE LEADER'S EXPECTATIONS

Our task isn't only to manage the expectations of our employees and customers; it's also to manage our own. In my first years as a leader, my vision often outpaced reality, and I got discouraged. A friend suggested I spend a month reading the book of Proverbs in the Bible. There are 31 chapters, so I could read a chapter a day. About two weeks into this venture, I came across a verse that at first seemed totally irrelevant: "Where there are no oxen, the manger is clean, but abundant crops come by the strength of the ox."[54]

I grew up in suburb of Atlanta, so the only animals in our neighborhood were dogs and cats, as well as some raccoons and squirrels. I have no personal experience with farm animals like oxen, but I sensed this verse had something to say to me. My wife Laura more than compensates for my lack of experience with farm animals. She grew up in a rural part of southern Georgia. In high school she was a member of FFA, and she showed pigs at agricultural events (although she hates it when I tell this story). Through her eyes, I began to understand the meaning of the verse.

The passage contrasts two different farms. The first one has no oxen to plow the fields and turn the grinding wheel. The manger, the eating trough, is clean. The farmer doesn't have to haul feed, and he doesn't need to shovel manure (or smell it). The barn is pristine, but the farm is unproductive. On the second farm, the owner employs the power of an ox to plant and harvest "abundant crops," but there's a cost: he has to lug feed to the trough and clean the barn of manure. The inherent questions the writer is asking are these: Are the farmer's profits worth the labor expended to use the strength of the oxen? Is the payoff worth the cost? And the implied answer is yes. The growth is worth it.

Some of us want success, but we have a "low crap tolerance." We want the benefits without the messiness and the work. At times I have longed for my job as a leader to be simple, streamlined, and clean . . . no mess at all. But that's not the way progress happens. I'm learning to have a much higher "crap tolerance," enlisting the work of people who bring their strengths to our mission, but knowing the work will get messier and there will be sometimes be stuff I need to clean up. In other words, we can expect plenty of junk on the journey to success.

When Garrett and I started ADDO, the two of us did it all. We created the curriculum, set up appointments, scheduled events, and delivered the content. But we reached only a handful of people. Since then, our staff has grown, our revenue has increased, our profit is larger, and our impact on people has grown exponentially, but it's

> **We can expect plenty of junk on the journey to success.**

messy on our "farm." I have to continually point people to our purpose (that's the feeding part) and wade in to resolve disagreements (that's the crap). Our systems and processes are more complex, and our accounting requires more of my time so I can stay on top of things. The added work isn't anyone's fault or a flaw of leadership; it's just the way organizations (and farms) thrive. We were reaching a few hundred people before, and now we're reaching nearly 100,000 annually across our programs. Is it worth it? You bet it is.

If my team and I don't understand the meaning of this proverb, we won't reach our goal of inspiring 500,000 leaders a year by 2020. With more impact, we'll need more oxen: more people, more programs, and more profit, which will inevitably produce more mess. This proverb has helped me view our problems in a very different way. They're not an intrusion in my job description as a leader; they're the cost I must pay for real progress.

CALLING AND THE CRITICS

Maybe it's just me. Maybe I'm the only one who gets sidetracked from progress by the carping of critics. Leaders have many different profiles, so I don't assume everyone is just like me, but humor me as I admit I am far too aware of criticism. After I spoke at an event for financial executives, the person in charge of the conference reviewed all the feedback and said, "Kevin, your talk was rated higher than any speaker we've ever had at our events . . . ever." Wow, that was encouraging. She gave me the compilation of the feedback from those at the event, and reading through them I found two negative comments out of about 400 people. I blocked out the 398 and focused on the two. I read them over and over again, fixated on the complaints, wondering how I could have done a better job. I imagined sitting down with those two to listen to them . . . no, actually to convince them to change their evaluations!

This isn't an isolated occurrence for me. When I'm a commentator on CNN or Fox News, I read the tweets after the show. I always skirt past the positive and obsess on the negative, even if the weight of all the comments is overwhelmingly positive.

Last year our company's customer retention was 96 percent. That's great, but you can guess where my attention focused. What were those four percent thinking of us . . . of me? What did I do wrong?

As I examine reviews of my speaking and our company, I try to draw a clear distinction between honest, corrective feedback and destructive criticism. I want to learn from one and ignore the other. Too often, however, I obsess over even the mildest and most good-natured constructive criticism, and I let harsh comments eat my lunch.

I have a choice, as we all do, of how to respond to feedback. Our calling—our purpose and all that drives us to have an impact on those around us—is far too important to let criticism crush us. I'm still struggling with this issue, so I keep these quotes close by:

> "If you just set out to be liked, you will be prepared to compromise on anything at anytime, and will achieve nothing" ("Iron Lady" Margaret Thatcher, the first female Prime Minister of Great Britain).

"The opposite of courage is not cowardice; it's conformity" (Jim Hightower, former Commissioner of Agriculture of Texas).

"Listen very carefully to the first criticism of your work. Note just what it is about your work the reviewers don't like; it may be the only thing in your work that is original and worth-while" (John Irving, novelist and Academy Award-winning screenwriter).

"You have enemies? Good. That means you've stood up for something, sometime in your life" (Winston Churchill).

"Let me never fall into the vulgar mistake of dreaming that I am persecuted whenever I am contradicted" (Ralph Waldo Emerson).

"Don't be distracted by criticism. Remember—the only taste of success some people have is when they take a bite out of you" (Zig Ziglar).

If we aspire to do something that really matters, we will have people who disagree with us, dislike us, and try to discredit us.

If we aspire to do something that really matters, we will have people who disagree with us, dislike us, and try to discredit us. Yes, I'm a card-carrying, people-pleasing, affirmation-seeking, applause-aholic. I'm trying to counter that tendency by leaning hard into wisdom, strength, and the security I find outside my performance, being convinced that the God of the universe delights in me whether others do or not. This perspective gives me a different lens to view the critics. I'm not as obsessed with them, so they don't hold as much power over me, and I can focus on my purpose and my calling.

Purpose must be far more than an abstract concept, a framed statement on a wall. It has to capture my mind and heart, energize my actions, and shape everything I do. When the purpose is clear, even the mundane becomes meaningful. If my purpose is too abstract, the criticism seems much more real, much closer, and devastating. My security and my calling are my anchors. If I lose those, I'm in big trouble. But when they are clear and strong, I can accept constructive feedback and ignore the harsh critics—and I'm much more likely to have the wisdom to tell the difference. If we have the right lens, we'll consider at least some of the criticism as confirmation that we're on the right road to our calling. Critics aren't necessarily our enemies, but they aren't the ultimate source of truth about us either. They have a role in sharpening and shaping us, but we need to remember: People don't build marble monuments to critics.

Change may be manageable, but progress is never guaranteed. Leaders, like it or not, are risk-takers who stand at the exciting intersection of the nine qualities we've examined in this book. If we clean off our lens so we can see more clearly, we'll have more confidence, lead with more passion, and genuinely care for the people around us. More than ever, we'll be people worth following. It's all a matter of perspective.

It's very easy to be different but very difficult to be better.
—Jonathan Ive

TAKE A LOOK...

1. How would you describe the differences between change and progress?

2. What is an example of "the herd effect" you've seen in leaders? What were the results of seeing change as the goal rather than progress?

3. Who is an example of a leader with "the igloo effect"? What were the results for the person's employees and company?

4. What are some ways you and your organization can measure outcomes instead of outputs?

5.   What is the damage of not managing expectations for customers, employees, and yourself? What are some practical things you can do to manage expectations more effectively for yourself, your team, everyone in your organization, and your customers?

6.   What are some practical things you can do to respond to your calling more than your critics?

7.   After reading this book, what are three specific, concrete steps you will take? Which one will you take first?

PICK UP THE LENS

I hope my talks and this book serve as a *mirror* to help leaders see themselves more clearly so that they can identify their greatest strengths and a couple of their current deficiencies. I hope what I've said and written is a *microscope* to help them see the intricacies of their motivations and desires, and I trust I've given them *binoculars* to get a vision of a better future after those perspectives change their lives.

When I speak to leaders about these nine shifts in perspective, they often ask me, "What do I do with all this information? I can't implement everything at once. Where should I start?" That's a great question. If you're also wondering, let me give you some suggestions.

First, pick one of the nine—the one that has captured your attention, the one you want to work on first. But don't rush to make immediate changes. Take plenty of time to think, ponder, and imagine what difference it will make for you and for your team if this perspective becomes an integral part of your life.

The first realization that I might have leadership abilities came out of the disaster with our Senior Class float at homecoming. Mr. Richardson saw something in me that I certainly hadn't seen. In that moment of my failure, he held up a mirror that reflected a very different message. I had seen only a goof-up, but he saw a young man with potential. I was discouraged, but he instilled hope and courage. His perspective proved to be a turning point in my life, but I still had a long way to go.

Seeing ourselves and our roles through a new lens opens a world of possibilities. A fresh perspective invites us to think, plan, dream, and relate to people in ways that are different from anything we've experienced before.

Second, when you have a vision of how acquiring and sharpening your perspective can make a difference in your life, write a plan. Make your goals ambitious, but reasonable. Establish clear action points and a timeline so you can measure your progress. Many people find the acronym SMART helpful when setting goals. They chart their new plan to be Specific, Measurable, Achievable, Relevant, and Time-bound.

Third, don't even think of doing this alone! Find a coach, mentor, friend, or colleague who will push you, pull you, encourage you, and kick you in the rear when you need it. You must be vulnerable enough to ask for help, but understand this: you're asking someone to invest time and attention in you that will multiply into the lives of every person you influence for the rest of your life. Whomever you select has a great opportunity to bet on you and make a difference.

Finally, realize that change is hard, so dig deep and be tenacious. Think of learning to live by the new perspective the same way you'd think of learning to play the violin or to play tennis. Learning any new skill feels terribly awkward at first . . . and maybe even wrong! But after a lot of practice, it becomes easier, and eventually it's really fun. The first months of seeing, thinking, and acting differently will feel strange. You'll play plenty of wrong notes and hit a lot of balls into the net or over the fence. But hang in there! Don't stop. The discipline is worth it.

As your first chosen perspective becomes second nature, you'll see the vision of it realized in your own life and in your leadership. Then it's time to tackle the next perspective, and this time you'll have more confidence that the process of growth and change will have a profound impact on your future.

Leadership is about helping others. As you acquire these new perceptions and skills, you'll impart them to the people around you. You'll be a servant leader, and your impact will continue to grow. That's why you're a leader, isn't it?

ENDNOTES

INTRODUCTION

1. "Restoring Eyesight with a Simple, Inexpensive Surgery," Bill Whitaker, *60 Minutes*, July 16, 2017, https://www.cbsnews.com/news/fighting-preventable-blindness-in-burma-and-beyond-2/

2. Experts in psychology and others who study human behavior explain that people naturally assume they are right: that a situation or a person's behavior must be the product of observable and easily identifiable causes. In other words, we attribute familiar causes to others' events and behaviors, whether they are accurate or not. This is called "attribution theory." For more, see https://www.psychologynoteshq.com/attributiontheory/

3. "Employee Engagement in U.S. Stagnant in 2015," Amy Adkins, Gallup, January 13, 2016.

4. David Moffet, "Removing the Onboard Terrorist from your Dental Office . . .," The Ultimate Patient Experience, November 28, 2013, https://theultimatepatientexperience.com/2013/11/28/removing-the-onboard-terrorist-from-your-dental-office/

5. The Arbinger Institute, *Leadership and Self-Deception* (San Francisco: Berrett-Koehler Publishers, 2010), p. xii.

CHAPTER 1

6. "Deloitte Study: Only 13 Percent of the US Workforce Is Passionate About Their Jobs," PR Newswire, June 7, 2017, https://www.prnewswire.com/news-releases/deloitte-study-only-13-percent-of-the-us-workforce-is-passionate-about-their-jobs-300469952.html

7. Nick Craig and Scott A. Snook, "From Impact to Purpose," *Harvard Business Review*, May 2014, https://hbr.org/2014/05/from-purpose-to-impact

8. "Engineer Who Opposed Challenger Launch Offers Personal Look at Tragedy," Researcher News, Langley Research Center, October 5, 2012, https://www.nasa.gov/centers/langley/news/researchernews/rn_Colloquium1012.html

9. Diane Vaughan, *The Challenger Launch Decision: Risky Technology, Culture, and the Deviance at NASA* (Chicago: University of Chicago Press, 1996), Preface.

10. "MR-1: The Four-Inch Flight," p. 293.

11. Romans 12:15.

12. Os Guinness, *The Call*, (Nashville: Word, 1998), p. 4.

13. Rolf Dobelli, *The Art of the Good Life* (New York: Hachette Books, 2017), Chapter 1.

14. Patti Neighmond, "People Who Feel They Have a Purpose in Life Live Longer," NPR, July 28, 2014, https://www.npr.org/sections/health-shots/2014/07/28/334447274/people-who-feel-they-have-a-purpose-in-life-live-longer

CHAPTER 2

15. Greg McKeown, *Essentialism: The Disciplined Pursuit of Less* (New York: Crown Business, 2014), p. 16.

16. Donna Brighton, "How Can Priority Be Plural?" Brighton Leadership Group, April 5, 2016, http://www.brightonleadership.com/2016/04/05/can-priority-plural/

17. Anka Wittenberg, "3 Ways to Simplify Your Company Culture and Build Trust," Entrepreneur, https://www.entrepreneur.com/article/272148

18. Ben Fox Rubin and Roger Cheng, "Fire Phone one year later: Why Amazon's smartphone flamed out," C/Net, July 24, 2015, https://www.cnet.com/news/fire-phone-one-year-later-why-amazons-smartphone-flamed-out/

19. J. Randall Keene and Timothy J. McKibben, *A Better Way* (Friendswood, TX: Baxter Press, 2016), pp. 116-117.

20. Stephen J. Covey, *7 Habits of Highly Effective People* (New York: Simon & Schuster, 1989).

21. Philippians 3:12-14.

CHAPTER 3

22. Proverbs 18:21.

23. Timothy J. Keller with Kathy Keller, *The Meaning of Marriage* (New York: Riverhead Books, 2011), p. 44.

24. Timothy J. Keller, *The Timothy Keller Sermon Archive* (New York City: Redeemer Presbyterian Church), "Love and the Practical Graces," Practical Grace: How the Gospel Transforms Character, January 13, 2002.

25. The three types of kindness are adapted from Tim Keller's message, "Befriending Grace," January 27, 2002.

26. John Gardner, *On Leadership* (New York: The Free Press, 1990), p. 135.

27. Peggy Noonan, *What I Saw at the Revolution: A Political Life in the Reagan Era* (New York: Random House, 1990), p. 321.

28. Harrison Kratz, "Maximizing Millennials: The Who, How, and Why of Managing Gen Y," Kenan-Flagler Business School, University of North Carolina, June 24, 2013, https://onlinemba.unc.edu/blog/geny-in-the-workplace/

29. Valerie Strauss, "The surprising thing Google learned about its employees—and what it means for today's students," *The Washington Post*, December 20, 2017, https://www.washingtonpost.com/news/answer-sheet/wp/2017/12/20/the-surprising-thing-google-learned-about-its-employees-and-what-it-means-for-todays-students/?utm_term=.6d57e6193d90

CHAPTER 4

30. For more information about Kolbe Assessments, go to www.kolbe.com.

31. For more information about the WinShape Foundation, go to https://winshape.org

32. Robert Reiss, "How Ritz-Carlton Stays at the Top," Forbes, October 30, 2009, https://www.forbes.com/2009/10/30/simon-cooper-ritz-leadership-ceonetwork-hotels.html#39fe2b8c10b1

CHAPTER 5

33. Mark 8:36.

34. Daniel James, "9 Must-Know Millennial Shopping Trends & Marketing Strategies of 2017," Rakuten Marketing, January 11, 2017, https://blog.marketing.rakuten.com/affiliate/9-must-know-millennial-shopping-trends-of-2017

35. "The World Bank in China," The World Bank, http://www.worldbank.org/en/country/china/overview

36. Cited by David Brooks in "Capitalism for the Masses," *New York Times*, February 20, 2014, https://www.nytimes.com/2014/02/21/opinion/brooks-capitalism-for-the-masses.html

37. David Brooks, "The Power of Altruism," *New York Times*, July 8, 2016, https://www.nytimes.com/2016/07/08/opinion/the-power-of-altruism.html

38. These quotes and others are cited at The Purpose Effect: Inspiring Quotes about a Higher Purpose, May 7, 2016, http://www.danpontefract.com/inspiring-ceo-quotes-about-a-higher-purpose/

CHAPTER 6

39. Robert Greenleaf, "The Servant as Leader," p. 6, Greenleaf Center for Servant Leadership, https://www.essr.net/~jafundo/mestrado_material_itgjkhnld/IV/Lideran%C3%A7as/The%20Servant%20as%20Leader.pdf

40. Adapted from Tim Keller, "A Counter-Culture of Grace," January 10, 2010, https://gospelinlife.com/downloads/a-counter-culture-of-grace-6035/

41. "Letter from the Birmingham Jail," cited in *The Atlantic*, August 1, 1963, https://www.theatlantic.com/politics/archive/1963/08/martin-luther-kings-letter-from-birmingham-jail/274668/

42. Marcel Schwantes, "The World's 10 Top CEOs (They Lead in a Totally Unique Way)," *Inc.*, March 29, 2017, https://www.inc.com/marcel-schwantes/heres-a-top-10-list-of-the-worlds-best-ceos-but-they-lead-in-a-totally-unique-wa.html

43. Ibid

44. All of these quotes are cited by Marcel Schwantes in "25 Unique Leadership Quotes to Inspire and Motivate," *Inc.*, February 22, 2016, https://www.inc.com/marcel-schwantes/25-unique-leadership-quotes-to-empower-both-leaders-and-followers.html

45. Viktor Frankl, *Man's Search for Meaning* (Boston: Beacon Press, 1959), p. 66.

CHAPTER 7

46. Andy Stanley, *Making Vision Stick* (Grand Rapids: Zondervan, 2007), pp. 19, 21.

47. Cited on WordStream, "23 Brilliant Marketing Quotes You Wish You'd Said," December 19, 2017, https://www.wordstream.com/blog/ws/2015/12/09/marketing-quotes

48. Jim Collins, *Good to Great* (New York: HarperBusiness, 2001), p.13.

49. Luke 12:48.

CHAPTER 8

50.   "5 Lessons from Undercover Boss," Mark Kolakowski, *the balance*, February 18, 2017, https://www.thebalance.com/undercover-boss-lessons-1287060

51.   Doug Dietz, "Transforming healthcare for children and their families," TEDx San Jose, CA, 2012, https://www.youtube.com/watch?v=jajduxPD6H4

52.   Roger Dooley, "The Most Common (And Dangerous) Market Research Mistake," *Forbes*, August 21, 2013, https://www.forbes.com/sites/rogerdooley/2013/08/21/market-research-mistake/#106b74073fe1

CHAPTER 9

53.   Steve Denning, "Measuring What Matters: From Outputs to Outcomes," *Forbes*, February 27, 2011, https://www.forbes.com/sites/stevedenning/2011/02/27/measuring-what-matters-from-outputs-to-outcomes-part-2/#2cfae39377e8

54.   Proverbs 14:4.

ACKNOWLEDGEMENTS

First and foremost, I'm grateful for those in my family who support me every step of the way: my wife Laura, my parents, Jeff and Lynne, and my sister Whitney, brother-in-law Jon, and my favorite nephews Kaden and Logan. I'm also thankful for my Uncle Mark, mother-in-law Kim, and the rest of my extended family.

This book would simply not have happened without the help and encouragement of many people. In particular, I want to thank . . .

. . . Pat Springle, who is an incredible writer, publisher, and friend.

. . . Marjorie Roberson, who helps me communicate my thoughts clearly through a weekly blog.

. . . Brittani daCamara, who helps share these messages across multiple platforms.

. . . Garrett Gravesen, my business partner and co-conspirator who always reminds me, "If it's not WOW, it's not worth doing!"

I would also like to thank the ADDO team for helping inspire people today to make impact tomorrow: Jackie Staley, Laura Engelbrecht, Elizabeth Jay, Rosy Harvey, Patrick McConn, Holly Connell, Christian Rich, Abbie Montgomery, Jake Lacy, Lindsay Corris, Linda Cottrell, Brooks and Laura Bradway, and the others who are on this journey with us.

Special recognition to Taylor Jones, Eric Brown, and the Whiteboard team, to Dan Duncan, Carson Nyquist and the Oust crew, and to Billy Boughey and Elevate.

To the great folks at Chick-fil-A, including Rodney Bullard, Ann Marie Mortaitakis, Jessica Purser, Matt Lingerfelt, Melonie Flavin, John

Mattioli, Mark Miller, David Salyers, L. J. Yankosky, Tim Tassopoulos, Evan Karanovich, John Stephenson, and the Cathy family. I'm grateful for your partnership to impact leaders across America.

There are a few pastors who are especially instrumental in my life, including Mike Linch, Johnny Foster, and Justin Holcomb.

Finally, I want to acknowledge the impact of those who have inspired me on my journeys abroad, especially Paulus and Marlieyse Wiratno in Indonesia.

To all of you, I am profoundly grateful.

LEADING A TEAM USING
THE LENS OF LEADERSHIP

This book is designed for individual study and team interactions. The best way to absorb and apply these principles is for each person to individually study and answer the questions at the end of each chapter then to discuss them in a team meeting.

Each chapter's questions are designed to promote reflection, application, and discussion. Order enough copies of the book for each person to have a copy.

A recommended schedule might be:

Week 1

Introduce the material. As the team leader, tell your story of how the principles in this book have shaped your perceptions of leadership.

Weeks 2–10

Start with the Introduction. Then, each week introduce the topic and share a story of how you've applied the principles. Lead people through a discussion of the questions at the end of the chapter. For the last week, include the conclusion in the reading and discussion.

PERSONALIZE EACH LESSON

Ask people in the group to share their responses to the questions that meant the most to them that week. Make sure you personalize the principles and applications. At least once in each group meeting, add your own story to illustrate a specific point.

FOCUS ON APPLICATION

The questions at the end of each chapter and your encouragement to group members to be authentic will help your group take big steps to apply the principles they're learning. Share how you are applying the principles in each week's chapter, and encourage group members to take steps of growth, too.

THREE TYPES OF QUESTIONS

If you have led discussions, you already understand the importance of using open questions to stimulate discussion. Three types of questions are *limiting, leading,* and *open.* Many of the questions at the end of each lesson are open questions.

- *Limiting questions* focus on an obvious answer, such as, "What is the research finding on page 47?" They don't stimulate reflection or discussion, but they can be a helpful beginning. If you use questions like these, follow them with thought-provoking, open questions.

- *Leading questions* require the listener to guess what the leader has in mind, such as, "Why is this research important to our team and our company?" The teacher who asks a leading question has a definite answer in mind. Instead of asking this kind of question, you should just refer to the concept and ask an open question about the point you have made.

- *Open questions* usually don't have right or wrong answers. They stimulate thinking, and they are far less threatening because the person answering doesn't risk ridicule for being wrong. These questions often begin with "Why do you think . . .?" or "What are some reasons that . . .?" or "How would you have felt in that situation?" or an open invitation: "Tell me more of what you're thinking."

PREPARATION

As you prepare to teach this material in a group or class, consider these steps:

1. Carefully and thoughtfully read the book. Make notes, highlight key sections, quotes, or stories, and complete the reflection section at the end of each chapter. This will familiarize you with the entire scope of the content.

2. As you prepare for each week's discussion, read the corresponding chapter again and make additional notes.

3. Tailor the amount of content to the time allotted.

4. Add your own stories to personalize the concepts and add impact.

5. Some discussions won't result in tidy conclusions. That's perfectly fine. Give people time to think about important topics and open the discussion again the next week.

6. People will get more out of the team's discussions if they read the chapter and personally answer the questions each week. Order books at least a week or two before you plan to begin so people will have time to get started.

ABOUT THE AUTHOR

Kevin Paul Scott has traveled to six continents and spoken to leaders from more than 100 countries. Kevin is the co-founder of ADDO, a leadership consultancy based in Atlanta, Georgia. ADDO exists "to inspire people today to impact tomorrow."

ADDO partnered with Chick-fil-A to create Chick-fil-A Leader Academy, a national program focused on impact through action.

Prior to founding ADDO, Kevin's background included non-profit charitable work, business ventures, and politics. After graduating from the University of Georgia, Kevin served on a presidential campaign team and then worked as a representative for a United States Congressman.

In consecutive years, Kevin was named to the "40 under 40" lists for *Georgia Trend* and then the *Atlanta Business Chronicle*. He is the author of three books.

For his leadership and business acumen, Kevin has been featured on Fox News, CNN, MSNBC, and in numerous publications, including *The New York Times, Washington Post,* and *Los Angeles Times.*

For fun, Kevin has been cage diving with Great White Sharks in South Africa, trekked Mountain Gorillas in Uganda, and ridden a llama in Colombia. However, he most enjoys being at home to cheer on the Atlanta Braves and Georgia Bulldogs. Kevin was raised in Kennesaw, Georgia, and is active in his local church. Known for his grassroots appeal and southern charm, Kevin speaks extensively at businesses, to educators, and within the faith community. He and his wife Laura live in Marietta, Georgia.

With Fredricka Whitfield on CNN

ABOUT ADDO

ADDO is Latin for "inspire."

ADDO WORLDWIDE

ADDO is a leadership consultancy. ADDO builds leadership programs, products, and experiences that inspire and equip individuals, teams, and organizations to lead well in society.

Through ADDO's innovative engage-expose-equip development model, they have partnered with some of the most well-respected companies to implement programs inside and outside of their organizations, including strategic business initiatives, educational programs, and effective employee engagement strategies.

ADDO has been recognized as one the "Best Places to Work" by the Atlanta Business Chronicle.

ADDO INSTITUTE

ADDO Institute is ADDO's 501(c)(3) not-for-profit arm that inspires people today to impact tomorrow through global leadership, student leadership, and thought leadership programs.

The ADDO Team

With Coach Vince Dooley

RESOURCES

To order copies of Kevin's books, go to www.KevinPaulScott.com

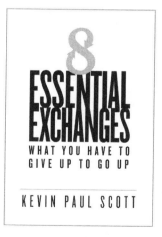

Exchanges aren't about choices between good and bad decisions. Those are easy. The most important exchanges are between really good things and even better things. Those are much harder, but they shape our lives in disproportionate ways.

In this book, Kevin Paul Scott identifies eight clear—and challenging—choices. He calls them "exchanges" because we give up something important when we choose something even more important. These are choices that confront every person almost every day. When we make them, we experience more fulfillment and have a greater impact than we ever dreamed possible.

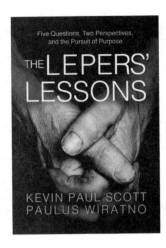

Four people had no status, no resources, and only a faint ray of hope that something good could happen to them, but they found the courage to take a step in the dark, into the desert, and into a destiny they never dreamed possible. *The Lepers' Lessons* is an ancient story that remains relevant today. The five questions the men inherently ask—and they invite us to ask—clarify our motives, give us direction, and fill us with hope that our lives can make a difference. Kevin Paul Scott and Paulus Wiratno come from different continents, different cultures, and different perspectives, but together, they give us a rich, deep grasp of our true purpose.